Judaism, Christianity, and Liberation

An Agenda for Dialogue

Edited by Otto Maduro

ORBIS BOOKS

Maryknoll, New York 10545

The Catholic Foreign Mission Society of America (Maryknoll) recruits and trains people for overseas missionary service. Through Orbis Books, Maryknoll aims to foster the international dialogue that is essential to mission. The books published, however, reflect the opinions of their authors and are not meant to represent the official position of the society.

Copyright © 1991 by Orbis Books
Published by Orbis Books, Maryknoll, N.Y. 10545
All rights reserved
Manufactured in the United States of America

Library of Congress Cataloging-in-Publication Data

Judaism, Christianity, and liberation: an agenda for dialogue /
    edited by Otto Maduro.
        p. cm.
    Includes bibliographical references.
    ISBN 0-88344-693-6
    1. Judaism—Relations—Christianity—1945- 2. Christianity and
other religions—Judaism—1945- 3. Liberation theology. 4. Judaism
and social problems. 5. Jewish-Arab relations—Religious aspects.
    I. Maduro, Otto, 1945-
BM535.J8284 1991
261.2'6—dc20   90-22940
                                                        CIP

To Frances Greenspoon,
Luis Mandoki, and
Manuelite Zelwer ...
they should know why

Contents

Preface   vi
Otto Maduro

Introduction: Liberation Theology and Judaism   1
Judd Kruger Levingston

Part I
LATIN AMERICAN PERSPECTIVES

1. Liberation Theology   23
   A Political Expression of Biblical Faith
   Leonardo Boff

2. Jewish and Christian Liberation Theology   33
   Pablo Richard

3. The Holocaust and Liberation   40
   Julio de Santa Ana

Part II
A JEWISH THEOLOGY OF LIBERATION?

4. Breaking the Chains of Necessity   55
   An Approach to Jewish Liberation Theology
   Michael Lerner

5. A Jewish Journey through Nicaragua   65
   Phyllis B. Taylor

6. God's Joke   73
   The Land Twice Promised
   Arthur Waskow

Part III
A CRITICAL DIALOGUE:
JEWISH AND CHRISTIAN PERSPECTIVES

7. **False Messianism and Prophetic Consciousness**   83
Toward a Liberation Theology of Jewish-Christian Solidarity
Rosemary Radford Ruether

8. **Jews, Israel, and Liberation Theology**   96
Richard L. Rubenstein

9. **God's Pain and Our Pain**   110
How Theology Has To Change after Auschwitz
Dorothee Sölle

10. **Economics and Liberation**   122
Can the Theology of Liberation Decide Economic Questions?
Norman Solomon

Postscript: Jews, Christians, and Liberation Theology   141
A Response
Marc H. Ellis

Contributors   151

Preface

OTTO MADURO

How utterly mistaken is the view that would isolate Nazism and its supreme expression, bureaucratic mass murder and the bureaucratically administered society of total domination from the mainstream of Western culture.

Richard Rubenstein, *The Cunning of History*

In 1987 Orbis Books, well-known for its publication of Third World liberation theologies, published two books by Jewish scholars: *On Earth as It Is in Heaven: Jews, Christians, and Liberation Theology* by Dan Cohn-Sherbok, and *Toward a Jewish Theology of Liberation* by Marc Ellis. In different ways, both of these books argued that liberation theology represents a constructive new avenue in Jewish-Christian dialogue. In the case of the work by Marc Ellis (which was later updated in light of the Palestinian uprising, or *intifada*), the argument was made that liberation theology offers a vital resource for the renewal of Judaism itself by recalling Jews to the prophetic heart of their tradition in solidarity with the world's poor — especially with those who are the special victims of Jewish empowerment, the Palestinians.

These arguments have stimulated a variety of responses. While some Jewish voices have been raised in support of the project of a Jewish liberation theology, others have been sharply critical. Many Jews, as a matter of fact, have raised serious doubts about whether liberation theology represents any progress at all in terms of Jewish-Christian relations; Latin American liberation theologians are charged with perpetuating anti-Semitic attitudes, or with "coopting" Hebrew scripture in a new version of Christian supersessionism. For some Jews the issue is not so much theological as having to do with the social and political implications of this theology, particularly the attitude of its advocates toward the State of Israel, or the relative silence of liberation theologians before the historical suffering of the Jews.

The present volume was conceived as an effort to advance this discussion from a number of perspectives. Unfortunately, what follows is not a true dialogue. The contributors were not able to respond to one another. Instead they are responding to an invitation that went out to a number of Jews and Christians, both Latin Americans and North Americans (and one European theologian) to consider these questions: What are the implications of liberation theology for the future of Jewish-Christian dialogue; and what are the implications of this dialogue for the future of liberation?

Although their work was the occasion for this discussion, Latin American theologians themselves had rarely addressed these questions. We are particularly pleased that several of them recognized the importance of this invitation and responded positively.

In soliciting responses from other contributors we discovered a range of difficulties that had to be confronted both by prospective Jewish and Christian authors. Nevertheless, in the time since this project was first conceived two current events or situations have underlined the timeliness and relevance of this discussion.

One is the ongoing debate—particularly vivid in Latin America—regarding the appropriate way to mark the imminent quincentennial of the Iberian-Catholic entry in the Americas in 1492. This discussion has, among other things, opened new light on the relation between Jews and Christians in the Americas. It so happens that 1492 also marks one of the high tides in the history of Christian persecution of the Jews—the year of the expulsion of all the Jews from Spain. This crusade against the Jews was carried out by the same people and with the same theological rationale and in the very same sweeping movement that initiated the massive occupation, enslavement, and genocide of the native African and American peoples.

Speaking personally, I should say that for me—as for many other Latin Americans—this is a crucial juncture. I am the son of a *marrano*—a Sephardic Jew whose family was forcibly converted to Catholicism under Iberian rule. My father's family was the first Jewish family in Venezuela—sometime toward the middle of the last century—after three-and-a half centuries fleeing from pogroms and poverty. In Venezuela they faced further pogroms and poverty until the poorer branch of the family, sometime in the 1870s, finally gave in and converted to Catholicism.

I share the hope that these "quincentennial times" might pose the occasion for a deeper reflection on our past, not only prompting greater awareness of the common legacy of suffering uniting Jews, Native Americans, and African Americans in this continent, but a keener critique, as well, of the roots of that injustice in Christian power, triumphalism, and supersessionism.

Another circumstance, prominent in the news as I write, is the struggle between the state of Israel and the occupied Palestinian territories—further complicated by the current war in the Persian Gulf. The state of Israel is a central symbol of survival to the Jewish people; its defense has often been a litmus test for Christian solidarity with Jews. Undoubtedly, however, the cost of Israeli empowerment in terms of the oppression of the Palestinian people represents one of the critical issues in any Jewish-Christian dialogue convened around the challenge of liberation theology. Latin Americans, furthermore, are especially sensitive to such issues as the Israeli contribution to the Nicaraguan contras, to the apartheid regime in South Africa, and to the Guatemalan military dictatorship.

Not all these issues are addressed by our contributors. In some ways this volume is only the tentative opening to an ongoing discussion. The project was begun before the collapse of the Eastern bloc regimes in Europe or the full flowering of the *intifada* in the Middle East—not to mention the outbreak of war in the Persian Gulf. There was no opportunity to expand the discussion to cover such issues as the resurgence of anti-Semitism in Eastern Europe or the emergence of a Palestinian liberation theology (see *Justice and Only Justice: A Palestinian Theology of Liberation* by Naim Ateek, Orbis Book, 1989), or the collapse of Marxist socialism throughout the world. These issues must form the basis of future discussion.

I would like to join the editors of Orbis Books in thanking all the contributors to this volume for addressing the issues in a frank and honest way. Our hope would be that this discussion might not simply advance the cause of dialogue between Jews and Christians, but contribute in some way to building a more just and peaceful life on this common earth of which we are a part.

INTRODUCTION

Liberation Theology and Judaism

Judd Kruger Levingston

The remarkable growth and momentum of liberation theology over the last two decades has captivated many in the Jewish community. Among Christian theologies that have emerged since World War II, liberation theology is unique not only because of its political implications, but also because it finds much of its inspiration from the five books of Moses (the Torah) and from Jesus' Jewish roots. In echoing Jewish values of community, justice, and freedom from oppression—even using language and metaphors familiar to Jews—liberation theology could provide the basis for a meeting ground for new forms of interreligious discussions.

A Jewish response to liberation theology needs to take into account three areas of concern. For Jews, the central question posed to liberation theology asks what it says about Jews, Judaism, and Israel.

Before exploring the liberationist Christian understandings of "liberation," it is worthwhile to explore Jewish conceptions of liberation through Jewish history and texts. Traditional sources show that much of Jewish philosophy and practice derive their meaning from the moment of liberation from Egypt. In this respect, liberation theology is consonant with Judaism; an exploration of its Jewish roots would amplify common theological themes.

JUDAISM AND LIBERATION

The Exodus has informed Jewish thought deeply since biblical times. The Ten Commandments begin with the memory of enslavement: "I the Lord am your God who brought you out of the land of Egypt, the house of bondage: You shall have no other gods besides Me."[1] The exodus experience is woven throughout the Torah with Egypt as a constant reminder of experiences of powerlessness. Daily prayers, too, link the Israelite crossing of the Reed Sea with praise for God, lauded as *Gaal Yisrael*—the Redeemer of Israel.

In the prophetic view, the Exodus is a paradigm for God's relationship with the Jewish people. The prophet Jeremiah foresees a time when all people bear the same high level of ethical responsibility as the priests.[2] Following the destruction of the first temple, Jeremiah depicts a renewal of the covenant, one that might build on that of the Exodus:

> It will not be like the covenant I made with their fathers, when I took them by the hand to lead them out of their land of Egypt, a covenant which they broke ... But such is the covenant I will make ... : I will put My Teaching into their inmost being and inscribe it upon their hearts.[3]

Jeremiah envisions a time when the covenant would penetrate the spirit. The prophet Isaiah also calls for a transformation in communal memory so that the responsibilities of covenant are not forgotten. He calls upon all to build society:

> I created you, and appointed you a covenant people, a light of nations—opening eyes deprived of light, rescuing prisoners from confinement, from the dungeon those who sit in darkness.[4]

The Passover Seder, arguably the most ancient annual rite performed continuously in the Western world, has elements of liberationism deeply embedded in its liturgy. The first-century rabbis determined that the Seder should be imbued with history, and they instruct in the Mishnah[5] that Jews should always comport themselves as if they, too, had been liberated from Egypt. To set the scene for this drama, the traditional text of the Haggadah recounts the Passover story beginning with an account of the humiliation and it ends with praise for God. Physical and spiritual humiliation frame the beginning of the Seder: the physical humiliation of slavery in Egypt (*avadim hayinu*) and the spiritual humiliation of paganism and idolatry (*mitkhilah ovdei zara hayu avoteinu*) remind us of an unhappy and uncomfortable past. The joyous conclusion of the service incorporates psalms of praise for God, including Psalm 114, the psalm that exults in the liberation from Egypt.

The activist theologians of today have antecedents in second-century Judea (present-day Israel). The Haggadah recounts a night when five rabbis spent a night at Bene Barak reclining together, "telling about the departure from Egypt all night." Their discussion was so animated that the rabbis had abandoned all sense of time until a student arrived to remind them that it was time for morning prayers. Scholars suggest that the rabbis' discussion was not an idle retelling of the Exodus: since Rabbi Akiva, one of the five, played such an important role in the Bar Kokhba rebellion of the year 132, the liberation from Egypt may have been the basis for a passionate discussion about liberation from Roman rule, the most pressing contemporary issue for Palestinian Jews.[6] If this is the case, then we may infer that the Exodus was as much an impetus for praxis then as it is now. Even if this was not the precise historical case, we may still understand why the liberation theologians are so passionate about the meaning of the Exodus for today.

Jesus, a first-century Palestinian Jew, probably shared the rabbinic understanding of the Exodus. Reenacting the Passover Seder at the Last Supper, Jesus demonstrated the importance of Passover and the Exodus in his understanding of personal transformation and liberation. The blessings over the bread and wine later became the symbols for his followers of the new covenant he personified. Although Jews do not believe Jesus was offering a new covenant, the symbolism of the eucharist, the bread and wine, are familiar. The Jewish symbols of covenant follow from the Passover and the Exodus, while the symbols of the Christian covenant follow from the Last Supper—Jesus' Passover—and the crucifixion.

A strong link between the covenant and compassion for the poor pervades Jewish thought. The idea of a "preferential option for the poor," however, reads differently for the Jewish people. Jews are instructed in the book of Exodus, "You shall not wrong a stranger or oppress him, for you were strangers in the land of Egypt."[7] Both Exodus 22:24 and Deuteronomy 15:7-8 demand a high level of charity toward needy kinsmen or to any who may be a "needy person among you." The Jewish sages conclude that charity begins among one's own people, but that it must extend to non-Jews as well.[8] The Torah demands justice on behalf of the poor, cautioning at the same time that justice on their behalf must not mean overcompensation or a blanket preference given to them in disputes. Exodus 23:2-3 instructs, "You shall neither side with the mighty to do wrong . . . nor shall you show deference to a poor man in his dispute." Passages concerning widows and orphans call both for charity and justice. So that evenhanded justice might prevail, their disputes must not be weighted differently. One should neither be too harsh nor too lenient.

Jewish ethics are rooted in a solidarity with the poor, to use the liberationist term, that is linked to the covenantal relationship with God. When God tells Moses that they shall serve God after leaving Egypt,[9] the medieval commentator Rashi explains that God's purpose in freeing the Israelites is to enable them to accept their destiny of receiving the Torah at Mount Sinai. The early rabbis explained God's rationale in *Midrash Rabbah*:

> When you ask Me, by what merit shall I bring them out of Egypt? Know that it is for the sake of the Torah which they will receive on this mountain from thy hands that they will go forth from here.[10]

As much as the Jews may have been elected to receive God's revelation, they also elected to assume the responsibility of following that revelation through the dutiful performance of mitzvot or commandments. In the Talmud, the rabbis discuss how one should fulfill the mitzvot concerning charity and deeds of loving kindness (*Gemilut Hasadim*). "Charity can be done only with one's money, but *Gemilut Hasadim* can be done with one's person and one's money."[11] *Zedakah*, the Hebrew word for charity, refers not only to alms, but also to justice. Jewish activism and sympathy with liberation movements have been informed not only by concepts of biblical justice, but also by the concept of *zedakah* from ancient times to our own day.

Medieval and modern rabbis concerned with society have tried to understand how a world damaged by hatred and war could be rebuilt. Their theology of *tikkun* describes God's apparent withdrawal from the day to day workings of society, leaving human beings in charge of their own condition. The repair of the world, they affirmed, will not take place through divine fiat as it did during biblical times, but it will take place only through human deeds and hard work. In a world undergoing its repair, justice ensures that those with power do not abuse those who lack it. For liberationists, God is active, present in those deeds. For Jews, each individual must choose how to exercise power with compassion.

The Passover Haggadah not only affirms the revolutionary implications of the Exodus as a revelation of God's power, but it also shows how seriously the ancient rabbis took such transforming moments. Michael Walzer joins this ancient tradition, explaining the revolutionary implications of the Exodus in modern terms of social analysis. In *Exodus and Revolution*, Walzer, a professor at the Institute for Advanced Study in Princeton, writes that Jewish liberation in the Exodus came not in the first exultant moments of crossing the Sea of Reeds, but much later in the status of a people in covenant with God; Jews are empowered by their own "radical voluntarism." In stating, "We will do and we will obey,"[12] Walzer writes that this voluntarism provides the impetus for activism:

Who would take the required risks, who would march into the wilderness or challenge the "giants" of Canaan, without some sense of an assured future? ... At Sinai in any case, the people decide, and that implies that they have what they seemed to lack in Egypt, the capacity for decision.[13]

Jewish peoplehood provided a mission as well as responsibility. Like his Christian counterparts, Walzer's explanation of the Exodus concludes with an imperative demanding justice and freedom.

Rabbi Irving Greenberg, an Orthodox rabbi and head of the Center for Learning and Leadership, has written extensively on the implications of the Exodus on Jewish empowerment in the state of Israel. A Jewish liberation theologian, he writes of Jewish liberation in the Exodus, noting that it affects our understanding of empowerment today:

The final realization of the Exodus will take place in actual history and not in some other world or reality, [thus] the credibility and persuasive power of the promise of redemption rises and falls under the impact of historical events.[14]

For many Jews, the transforming events of this century, the Holocaust and the establishment of the state of Israel, mark turning points as significant for our own time and for all history as the Exodus.

In the Exodus, God was revealed as the liberator from spiritual and physical enslavement. In the Holocaust and the founding of the state of Israel, one might also find God revealed as the liberator from utter despair. Despite the political and economic freedoms Jews gained from emancipation in Europe and North America, the Holocaust showed that the world still considered the Jews powerless.[15] Zionism sought to liberate Jews from their powerlessness in Europe. Greenberg suggests that since taking power is an inescapable necessity after the Holocaust, the central challenge of this age for Jews is the attainment of power and the regulation of its use by covenantal ethics. He also argues that the achievement of a national state has changed Jewish identity by requiring each individual to engage in a self-critique of power:

How to use the power is the new halakhah, but denial or endangering the power is considered the unforgivable sin. In this era, which orients by the Holocaust and Israel, such a denial is the equivalent of the excommunicable sins of earlier eras: denying the Exodus and the God who worked in the Biblical age or denying the Rabbis and separating from Jewish fate in the Rabbinic era.[16]

Acknowledging that Jewish power in Israel is not always used morally, Greenberg criticizes the abuse of power while still insisting that empowerment itself is necessary. All governments make mistakes because they are human institutions, but the covenantal ethic is upheld by building in corrective mechanisms.[17]

Marc Ellis, a Jewish professor at the Institute for Peace and Justice at the Maryknoll School of Theology, is also developing a Jewish theology of liberation based on the transforming events of the Holocaust and the founding of the state of Israel. Ellis concentrates on the religious and political ideals Christians and Jews can share in this world. He is hopeful that "the Holocaust [can] become the catalyst for healing a brokenness that has plagued both communities for almost two thousand years."[18] The Holocaust is central to Ellis's thinking because it is the primary historical experience of this century that gives Jews empathy with today's powerless.

Ellis speaks of the Palestinian *intifada* and of the current political turmoil in the Middle East. He believes that liberation theology and the historical lessons of the Holocaust must be applied to Israeli-Arab politics. While many may disagree with that thesis, Ellis has taken liberation theology more deeply into the Jewish community. For him, the lesson of the Holocaust is not so much that Jewish empowerment is necessary for survival in the modern world, but that Jewish empowerment *obligates* self-criticism and solidarity with other oppressed and suffering peoples: a Jewish theology of liberation "affirms empowerment with the proviso that one must affirm the empowerment of others as well."[19]

For Ellis, the complement to Jewish empowerment is found in the Palestinian Arabs. He writes, "A true Jewish liberationist believes that Palestine and the support of a Palestinian state formed by the Palestine Liberation Organization need to be part of any discussion of Israel and thus part of the ecumenical dialogue."[20]

JEWISH CRITICISM

Liberation theology is beginning to influence some Jewish thinkers; yet, many are reluctant to join this movement because of the misunderstandings of Jews, Judaism, and Israel that find their way into many liberationist writings. It is significant that many liberation theologians live in areas where there are few Jews. When these theologians were students in Europe in the 1950s and early 60s, their theological studies reflected the prevailing Christian doctrine of supersessionism. Upon their return to work in peripheral regions of the world, traditional ideas persisted even while Catholic doctrine began to change in the late 1960s and 70s. Especially after the Second Vatican Council, the Catholic Church began to consider Jews and Judaism in a more fraternal manner.

In the vast literature written by liberation theologians, one may find statements about Jews or Judaism that have led some critics to consider it a new form of anti-Judaism.

Gustavo Gutiérrez, a Peruvian priest and theologian, was among the first to articulate a systematic liberation theology in his book *A Theology of Liberation* published in 1973. While his book was one of the most developed expressions of liberation theology to date, some of the theological terms represent a Judaism that seems weak and corrupt:

When the infidelities of the Jewish people rendered the Old Covenant invalid, the Promise was incarnated both in the proclamation of a New Covenant, which was awaited and sustained by the "remnant," as well as in the promises which prepared and accompanied its advent.[21]

This language unfairly denigrates the Jewish people. Some who have met Gutiérrez personally have spoken about his commitment to developing a better understanding of Judaism. One may hope that as his interest develops, he will repudiate such statements.

Naim Ateek, a Palestinian Christian theologian in Jerusalem, is also understanding of trends in Jewish history and changes in religious thought, especially since the establishment of the state of Israel. Yet, while his vision of a political settlement includes both a Jewish and a Palestinian state joined by common concerns,[22] his theology is much less understanding. He asserts that Jesus' inclusivity was greater than that of first-century Jews. He cites the first chapter of the Gospel of John:

[Jesus] came to his own home and his own people received him not. But to all who received him, who believed in his name, he gave power to become children of God; who were born, not of blood nor of the will of the flesh nor of the will of man, but of God.[23]

Ateek finds solace that Jesus "breaks through the pages of so many books of the Old Testament."[24] It demeans the validity and integrity of Judaism to imply that Jesus' charisma rests primarily in the failings of the Hebrew Bible. An alternative understanding of Jesus' charisma might be based on the message he offered, a promise of life in heaven to those who accepted him.

The Costa Rican theologian Victorio Araya shares an understanding with Jews that God is the *Go'el*, the rescuer and savior of the people.[25] In his book *God of the Poor*, Araya describes Jesus' discussions with the Pharisees. He implies that the Pharisees had no sense of God's transcendence, because of their emphasis on human traditions. He writes:

Jesus proclaims God's transcendence in his discussions with the Pharisees—for example, in accusing them of seeking to manipulate God through human traditions (Mark 7:1–17). His defense of that transcendence is all the more remarkable in that these traditions through which Jesus' interlocutors "nullify God's word," are religious traditions (Mark 7:13).[26]

What Araya fails to note is that those very Pharisaic traditions were neither monolithic nor empty and spiritless, but they were a means to God and to a transcendent relationshp with God. Jesus was not entirely alone in some respects. The idea of God as *Go'el* points to a time of redemption, an idea expressed in daily prayer today, and, we may suppose, an idea familiar to average Jews of the second temple period.[27]

The Pharisees also added a blessing to the daily liturgy, praising God for the resurrection of the dead.[28] While many of the Pharisaic party may have been as insincere as the New Testament suggests, in Josephus's *Antiquities* we find that the Pharisees ardently believed in the inevitability that good transcends evil, and that virtuous behavior is rewarded in a world to come.[29] By remaining limited to the narrative of the New Testament, Araya does not have a complete understanding of the beliefs of Pharisaic

Judaism. The New Testament portrayal of the Pharisees does not give a complete picture of beliefs at the time, especially concerning a transcendent relationship with God.

The Reverend John T. Pawlikowski, professor of social ethics at the Catholic Theological Union in Chicago, affirms much of what liberation theology teaches. He cautions that the liberation theologians need a more complete understanding of Jesus and Jewishness. He writes that contemporary sources would illuminate the basis for Jesus' compassion for the poor. Jesus, like the Pharisees, saw each individual as responsible for developing a relationship with God.[30] Jesus' entry into the Jerusalem temple highlighted his intolerance for corruption and for what he perceived as the blatant disregard for the poor. In entering the temple, he sought to restore its sacredness, not to destroy it.

Some liberationist writings are troubling for Pawlikowski. Jon Sobrino, professor of philosophy and theology in San Salvador, has written a christology denouncing first-century Judaism and its leaders. He writes that the Pharisees impose "intolerable burdens" on the peole.[31] In contrast, Jesus represents the only hope for the liberation of Israel. Pawlikowski asserts:

> What Sobrino seems to be saying is that this whole covenantal tradition can only be assessed as negative by the Christian believer; the Christ event destroyed any value or purpose it might have had previously.[32]

Pawlikowski, sensitive to the way Jewish sources are employed in liberationist writings, believes that liberation theology can be built on sources in the Hebrew Bible and the New Testament without the perpetuation of anti-Judaic elements.

Rabbi Leon Klenicki, director of the Department of Interfaith Affairs of the Anti-Defamation League of B'nai B'rith International, is a vociferous critic of liberation theology. He attacks it as a "teaching of contempt," which lacks an understanding of Judaism. For Jews, he explains, the mitzvot, the commandments from God, served as the foundation for the society created after the Exodus. By ignoring the mitzvot, the liberation theologians have not done justice to the depth of religious faith that link the Jewish people with God. Klenicki accuses the liberation theologians of abandoning the Jewish people after chapter 19 of the book of Exodus. Klenicki writes, "Liberation thinkers freeze Judaism at the time of leaving Egypt. It would seem that Jews are only Jews when enslaved."[33]

As liberation theologians point out, much of its innovation lies in that it is not bound by the same theological presuppositions of the northern European and North American theologians. Even with this consideration, it is difficult to ignore statements that denigrate Judaism, alienating potential Jewish sympathizers. In *Passion of Christ, Passion of the World*, Boff writes, "The Jews' rejection of Jesus, their stratagems, will be seen as a hardening of their hearts, a refusal to hear the voice of God speaking through Jesus."[34] Klenicki states, "This is worse than the church fathers!" He argues that their non-Western background should not justify their adherence to traditional teaching. Since many of these theologians were educated in Europe, they should be aware of recent positive changes in church teachings about Judaism.[35]

As a young movement, liberation theology has evolved considerably. For it to disregard the ancient Jewish tradition of liberationism seems a tragic sin of omission, leaving aside more than two thousand years of great thought, and it also leads to misunderstandings.

For Jews, the fundamental purpose of liberation was to become released into the covenantal relationship with God. When Latin American clergy met in Medellín, Colombia, in 1968 to formulate a religious response to the suffering of Latin American poor, they placed social and religious programs at the top of their agenda. Plans were made for the development of *comunidades eclesiales de base*, basic Christian communities. Their inspiration came both from the Hebrew Bible and from the life of Jesus. The bishops at Medellín couched their aspirations in biblical themes. Their conference concluded with an analogy to the exodus of the Israelites from Egypt:

> Just as Israel of old, the first people [of God], felt the saving presence of God when He delivered them from the oppression of Egypt, so we also, the new People of God, cannot cease to feel his saving passage in [the passage of all] from conditions of life that are less human, to those that are more human.[36]

This conference unequivocally affirmed that economic development alone could not ensure humane living conditions. Only a religious movement of liberation could build new communities as free as those that emerged after the exodus.

In Jewish theology, the importance and dignity of the poor did not singlehandedly bring about the Exodus. While Christian theologians equate the poor with those of the covenant, Jews separate the two. The bishops at Medellín called the poor "the new people of God." James Cone, professor of theology at Union Theological Seminary, writes, "Jesus's cross is God's election of the poor, taking the pain and suffering upon himself."[37] For Jews, however, the "preferential option for the poor" must be qualified. Professor Jon Levenson of the Harvard Divinity School explains that while the Torah sides with the powerless, "oppression, poverty, and suffering were not thought to qualify one for inclusion in the chosen people."[38] God heard the suffering of the enslaved Israelites, as one reads in the book of Exodus, and God *also* "remembered His covenant" (Exodus 2:24). It was the covenant that liberated the Israelites, not simply poverty or slavery.

For the Peruvian theologian Gutiérrez, the Bible is a revolutionary text.

He draws parallels between the ancient story and modern circumstances in a way Jews rarely do. For him, it is revolutionary because it describes God's preference for the powerless. For contemporary Christians, Israelite labor is a historical echo of their own backbreaking work, and the hardening of the pharaoh's heart is likened to the burgeoning strictures of international dependency and national debt.

When he proclaims "The exodus experience is paradigmatic,"[39] Gutiérrez is describing its use as a paradigm for Christians. He tends to define the Christian relationship to God as one that goes further than the Jewish relationship with God. Since the Exodus was an incomplete model of freedom from enslavement (tragedies continued to take place in the world), the continuation of the revolution must take place in Jesus. So, he writes, it is ultimately the "work of Christ"[40] that fulfills liberation and salvation. But Gutiérrez also links Jesus to the Jewish patriarch Abraham, who established the first covenant with God. Abraham's covenant, he writes, "is fulfilled in Christ. . . . In Him we are the 'issue' of Abraham, and so heirs by promise."[41] Thus the Jewish roots are at the same time affirmed, but quickly set aside.

George Pixley, an American Baptist who teaches in Mexico City, has published an interpretation and study of the book of Exodus. For Pixley, the exodus provided the catalyst for the reconstitution of the Israelites into a classless society, notable for its lack of kingship, bureaucracy, and private holdings. He asserts that Latin American Christians "read Exodus confidently as a revolutionary text,"[42] reading it as a call to overthrow the status quo. The achievement of the biblical Israelites remains significant as a model of social change, but Pixley's interpretations are at odds with those of Jewish tradition. Professor Levenson writes that Pixley's concern with finding meaning in the political situation and the role of the poor leads to a new form of supersessionism. He argues:

> The story of the Exodus has been rewritten under the pressure of the crisis of the poor in the Third World; now the Jews have been left out of their own foundational story, superseded by the poor and the oppressed, as they were once superseded by the communion of the baptized.[43]

Pixley's work provides an opportunity for discussion and potentially fruitful interreligious dialogue on the meaning of the biblical texts. Some, however, may find either the traditional Jewish position or Pixley's novel interpretation too remote even to enter into discussions.

Since 1965 Catholics have sought to redefine their understanding of Judaism through the legacy of the Second Vatican Council and especially in light of the document *Nostra Aetate*. In this document, the Catholic Church "repudiates" anti-Semitism, carefully articulating the "spiritual bond linking the people of the New Covenant with Abraham's stock." Without repudiating the significance of Christian faith in the "cross of Christ as the sign of God's all-embracing love," the church acknowledged that religions consist of universal truths.[44]

Harvard Divinity School professor Harvey Cox thinks that the propensity to supersessionism is waning. He adds that one can find worse examples in mainstream theological writings of the last twenty-five years.[45] Archeology and biblical scholarship have begun to persuade some Christian scholars, including liberation theologians, to abandon the claims that the relationship a Christian has with God is superior to that of a Jew. In his book *The Silencing of Leonardo Boff*, Cox writes that most liberation theologians "hold that Jesus can only be understood properly in *continuity* with the faith of Israel and in the light of the Hebrew Scripture."[46] Since liberation theology is about God's sympathy with the oppressed of all races and all religions, it is important that liberation theologians become more knowledgeable about Jews and Judaism. While it need not agree with Jewish tradition, it owes an intellectual debt to its theological origins.

Although it claims to embrace all the world's poor, liberation theology is not a generic theology of justice and social activism: it is distinctly Christian. Its origin lies both in the story of the Exodus and in the Christian cycle of death and resurrection. Jews rarely engage in the kind of systematic theology that the liberation theologians use. Liberation theologians are most concerned with bringing change to their own contexts. At the same time, though, they make general statements about the God of *all* the poor and about "the new people of God." Thus they write theologies that are both specific and universal. When statements emerge such as that of Segundo, "Every theology is political, even one that does not speak or think in political terms,"[47] the world is divided into two camps, oppressor and oppressed. There is an unfortunate tendency to dismiss critics simply as sympathizers with oppressors. For this reason, liberation theology occasionally tilts toward a new form of triumphalism. Victorio Araya, for example, states: "One's relationship with God comes to be expressed in one's relationship with the poor."[48] Without denying that one's relationship with the poor is a significant measure of one's ethics, are there not other ethical and political issues that also define one's relationship with God?

For those in the West who may wish to infer a plan of action for their own contexts or political concerns, it will be difficult. Although students of theologies of liberation are told to support the poor against the oppressor, reality shows that battle lines of oppressor and oppressed cannot be drawn so easily. In some conflicts, as in Lebanon, surrogate armies fight other surrogate armies. In the recent uprising in China, should we have sided with the government, the "people's government," or with the students who wanted changes in that revolutionary government? Would we side with the poor in Iran even if they seek another violent and intolerant ruler to reinstate the fervor of the Ayatollah Khomeini? Since these are largely political questions, not theological questions, liberation theologians may need to offer more direction on political issues, or may need to offer more insight into how communities should exercise justice.

The Jewish relationship with God is expressed both in one's inner faith and in one's behavior and commitments. Jews examine ethical issues, interpersonal relations, and religious behavior in the Talmud and codes. God's relationship with the Jews continues to be played out in daily behavior and in the continuing evolution of humanity. In contrast, for the liberation theologians, God's will seems to be made clearest in the success of a cataclysmic event such as a revolution.

One final area of concern has to do with liberationist attitudes toward Israel. While few liberation theologians speak of the state of Israel at all, many Jews are concerned that liberation theologians may look unfavorably on the existence of the state of Israel, given their socialist leanings and sympathies with movements of national liberation.

A great deal of literature has been written concerning the political and economic aspects of liberation theology. Many Jews such as Rabbi Leon Klenicki are sympathetic with the liberationist concern for the poor, but they believe socialism to be an inadequate solution to the problems of the Third World. Jews may be especially sensitive on this issue because they fear that movements of national liberation or national socialism will only lead to the kind of totalitarian regimes and anti-Semitic uprisings that have taken place in Nazi Germany, Stalinist Russia, and recently in the Soviet Union. The rampant anti-Semitism that often exists in these sorts of regimes is frightening.

David Singer, director of research, the American Jewish Committee, sees the decline of socialist states in current politics as a significant indicator. At a time in history when centrally controlled economics seem to be moving toward democratic reforms and toward freer forms of enterprise, the political inclinations of liberationists seem out of step.[49] As the Soviet Union undergoes *perestroika* and the Nicaraguan elections have brought a loyal opposition to power, the revolutionary vision of liberation theology may need to be revised. The poor might be "liberated" more effectively through the beginnings of communal and private enterprise and through alliances with the middle classes.

Jews look upon Israel as the culmination of their own national liberation and empowerment. Because Jews have experienced forms of oppression in this century in Europe and in countries as disparate as Ethiopia and Iraq, they may be both sympathetic to nationalist aspirations and guarded, fearful of its implications on Jewish life.

The publication of *The Wrath of Jonah* by the Catholic theologian Rosemary Radford Ruether and her husband, the political scientist Herman J. Ruether, represents the sort of asymmetrical critique of Israeli power that makes Jews feel scrutinized and, as a result, less willing to join progressive causes. The Ruethers write, for example:

To be concerned about Jewish suffering obliges one to be concerned about black South African suffering, women's suffering, the suffering of homeless refugee people in many parts of the world, and Palestinian suffering.[50]

A critique of the state of Israel need not necessarily be seen as evidence of anti-Semitism. The singling out of Jews for failing to offer universal sympathy is simply unfair. Jewish concern about Jewish suffering demonstrates strong intragroup solidarity and one should not imply that it is merely parochial or selfish. The call to be concerned about world suffering should be directed to *all* people who live comfortably. The pointed critique of Israeli power must join with a symmetrical critique of Arab power and the lack of sustained productive diplomatic assistance that might come to the Palestinian Arabs from strong Arab states. The sympathetic descriptions of Palestinian suffering must join with sympathetic descriptions of oppressed Soviet, African, and Jewish citizens who are denied basic rights in Arab countries.

Verses in Exodus chapters 22 and 23 demand that people give of themselves charitably. Exodus 23:3 is a reminder that justice does not mean overcompensation—each side must share the burden of peacemaking. For Greenberg, these verses are particularly important in the peace process. To enact the "option for the poor"—where "the poor" are the Palestinians—their rights need to be balanced with the full dignity and security of Israel and of the Jewish people. In Greenberg's view, the often negative attitude toward Jews and Judaism signals a more fundamental problem with liberation theology: that for the sake of the poor, injustices to others may be sanctioned by "liberators," only repeating the repression of totalitarian regimes.[51]

Because of their own historical experience with persecution, most Jews feel deeply concerned about the welfare of oppressed peoples. For the same reason, many are wary that their concern for "the other" might not be reciprocated. The failure of the West to contain the rise of Nazism and the Holocaust, the failure of the Allies to accept Jewish refugees in World War II, as well as the current barrage of anti-Israel sentiment coming from the developing world, leads many Jews to hesitate to embrace causes that might turn against them in the future.

Ultimately, if liberation theology is to reach a larger audience and achieve greater influence, it must strip away its supersessionism. If critics can see it as a theology of the faithful, and not as a prescription for totalitarianism, it will be a constructive step forward.

AGENDA FOR FUTURE DIALOGUE

Christian and Jewish liberationist thinkers have a great deal to offer each other in developing theologies of political activism. Solutions to the world's great problems frequently are thought to lie in the hands of those in power. Both Christianity and Judaism teach of the power of the individual to change both community and society at large to bring about social justice.

Liberation theology may be threatening to many Jews particularly because it concludes that political change must be accompanied by theological change. Marc Ellis believes a Jewish theology of liberation is necessary to ensure that Jews will reach lasting peace with Palestinian Arabs in the Middle East. He writes: "A political solution without a theological transformation simply enshrines the tragedy to be repeated again."[52] Ellis's call is urgent; yet very few Jews understand what a theological transformation might entail, because of the Jewish tendency to express theology not so much through systematic thought, but through community building and through new understanding of texts that may be two thousand years old.

Zionism, the movement to build a Jewish state in the land of Israel, became the national liberation movement of the Jewish people in the late nineteenth century. In *Der Judenstaat* [The Jewish state], written at the turn of the century, Theodor Herzl outlines a plan for a Jewish state that could take its place among other nations. Free of theocracy, spurred on by incentives for economic, cultural, and political development, Herzl envisions a democratic socialist state that could absorb and provide for new immigrants. He envisions a system of social welfare that would ensure that suitable living conditions would be provided for the poor,[53] and he outlines work relief programs to ensure that all would be able to earn a salary. Herzl drew a direct parallel between his Zionism and the exodus. He wrote:

> The founding of the Jewish State, as I envisage it, presupposes modern, scientific methods. If we journey out of Egypt today, this cannot be done in the simple fashion of ancient times.[54]

Herzl's model of national liberation was a blueprint for the modern Jewish society created in Palestine in the early part of this century.

Like liberation theology, Zionism is also a young movement on the world stage. Its history and current state should serve as a model of a liberation movement that has attained many of its stated goals. The establishment of a democratic government with a network of cooperative settlements, educational systems, hospitals, and social services have all taken place within half a century. Foreign contributions, many coming from diaspora Jewish communities, have helped Israel to develop its technological capabilities.

Critics of Zionism rightly point out some of its limitations, but it is instructive to look at its short history of practical experience. Christians who seek to apply theologies of liberation to their own contexts may see in Israeli history the ways in which ideology affects a nation's character, and the ways in which the "preference for the poor" may require a choice between the poor abroad and the poor who are closer to home. The practical implementation of ideology cannot always be consistent.

Since its early days, some Zionist thinkers spoke with conviction about the establishment of peaceful relations with Arab neighbors. When Judah Magnes wrote his essay "Like All the Nations?" in 1930, he presciently concluded, "The true parallels and balancing forces are Jews and Judaism on the one side, and the Arab peoples and even all of Islam on the other."[55] The philosopher Martin Buber also recognized the importance of Jewish-Arab cooperation. On the other hand, other Jewish thinkers joined the Zionist leader Vladimir Jabotinsky who sought an unequivocal Jewish majority power in Palestine. Jabotinsky stated, "Our demand for a Jewish majority is not our maximum — it is our minimum: it is just an inevitable stage if only we are allowed to go on salvaging our people."[56] Indeed many of Jabotinsky's ideological descendants wish for the "Greater Israel" he envisioned, but other equally fervent Zionists seek a democratic solution, a shared land and accommodation with the Palestinians.

Latin American liberation theologians have written very little about Zionism or about Israel,[57] probably because they are most concerned about issues and questions that relate to their own people. Nevertheless, many Jews are concerned that liberation theology will call for significant changes in Israel's identity as a Jewish national state. Most liberation theologians who have studied the Middle East — even Palestinians such as Naim Ateek — do not call for Israel's destruction: rather, they seek a Palestinian state alongside Israel in the West Bank and Gaza and, along with it, an end to claims for a "Greater Israel."

In terms of sheer volume, Jewish theology is scarce when compared to Christian theology. Some argue that Judaism cannot be described through the methods of theology because it is not rooted in defining the relationship through mitzvot and good deeds.[58] Yet, this very component of Jewish theology leads both Jews and Christians to agree that God wants people to form communities that ensure protection and sustenance for the weak and the poor. The Exodus provided a fundamental reference point in the relationship between God and the Jews. In the years since the Holocaust and the establishment of the state of Israel, politics has allowed the Jews to confront what it means to be both powerless and powerful. The experience of the Holocaust has led many to conclude that God does not intervene in history; rather, that liberation is in the hands of individuals acting on their own initiative.

Critics may wish to denigrate liberation theology by pointing to the failures of liberation movements across the world. Nicaragua, for example, faces continuing political and economic woes. On the other hand, the achievements in health care and education after the 1979 revolution were remarkable. The upheaval in Eastern Europe is remarkable and the trends toward democracy in South Korea are encouraging as well. In South Africa, the churches are at the center of nonviolent efforts to topple the system of apartheid there. Jewish peace activists in Israel and throughout the Jewish Diaspora join with Israeli Arab and Palestinian Arab activists, hoping that their friendship and mutual respect may lead to a large-scale political solution.

Liberation theologians favor participatory democracy with equal opportunity for involvement in political life. Professor Cox, who has written extensively on Boff's work, explains that Boff is not looking toward a theocracy: he is describing a "mild form of democratic socialism."[59] Although world politics seems to be moving toward Western-style democracy and democratic capitalism, thinkers on the right could come to see why socialist forms of government seem to be the logical solution to the economic and political structures in Latin America and elsewhere.

With this is mind, Jews and Christians need to address several issues in understanding each other's liberationism:

- Much of mainstream Christian theology has affirmed that the Jewish covenant with God exists side by side with the covenant of the Christians with God. Christian liberation theologians need to stop casting the Pharisees and first-century Judaism in a negative light. One further step is the substitution of the term "the Hebrew Bible" for the term "Old Testament."

- Jewish sources will add depth to any discussion of liberation because liberation is so fundamental to the Jewish ethos and to Jewish attitudes toward empathy with the poor. Equally important, the Bible and Talmud offer a model of how liberated slaves, after the Exodus, went on to become free and to create a free society. The God who joins with the suffering is the God of both Jews and Christians. By turning more frequently to Jewish biblical and rabbinic sources, liberationist writings will speak from an enriched vocabulary and repertory of liberation paradigms, and they will better understand the roots of Christian theology.

- One of liberation theology's strongest messages is that one must choose whether to side with oppressors or the oppressed. Polarizing language, however, may stifle conciliatory voices, bringing about a hardening of both critical and liberationist positions. In the middle ground, one attains perspective required to analyze or to create solutions for the problems of the day.

- Through interreligious dialogue, misperceptions can be overcome. Liberation theology is a young movement, and its understanding of Jews, Judaism, and Israel will continue to evolve. Just as Zionism has evolved from the time of Herzl, liberation theology has evolved since Medellín. Interreligious dialogue will address issues of concern in the future.

- Jews and Christians differ in their understanding of God and how God may intervene or inspire events as history is played out. They also differ in their understanding of God's covenant. These and other profound differences may persist. The clarification of those differences, however, may allow people of both religions to meet from a position of mutual respect, not from one of suspicion and mistrust.

• The Holocaust and Jewish empowerment in the state of Israel, as well as Jewish tradition, demand concern and action to alleviate the plight of peoples both inside and outside the Jewish community. Liberation theology may be one philosophy that draws communities of Jews together.

In regions where liberation theology is most popular, political and social exigencies work against conciliation. Unfortunately, the personal discussions that need to take place for Jews and Christians to understand each other may be difficult to convene. When these discussions take place, theologies of liberation may bring Jews and Christians to find shared religious grounding for principles of social welfare and the appropriate use of power. A failure to find common ground may ultimately prove to be an impediment to improved Jewish-Christian relations.

NOTES

1. Exodus 20:2–3. All biblical quotations come from The Jewish Publication Society, *Tanakh* (Philadelphia: Jewish Publication Society, 1985).
2. Michael Walzer, *Exodus and Revolution* (New York: Basic Books, 1985), p. 91.
3. Walzer, *Exodus*, p. 118, and Jeremiah 31:32–33.
4. Isaiah 42:6–7.
5. *Mishnah Pesahim* X:4. The Mishnah is a formal codification of Jewish law completed in the generations following the destruction of the second temple.
6. Nahum Glatzer, ed. *The Passover Haggadah* (New York: Schocken Books, 1989), pp. 27–29. Translations from Hebrew are the author's.
7. Exodus 22:20.
8. Nehama Leibowitz, *Studies in Shemot* (Jerusalem: World Zionist Organization, 1976), p. 408.
9. Exodus 3:12.
10. Dr. A. M. Silbermann, *Pentateuch with Rashi's Commentary*, vol. 2 (London: Shapiro, Vallentine, 1930), commentary on Exodus 3:12.
11. Babylonian Talmud, *Sukkah 49b* (London: Soncino Press).
12. Exodus 23:8.
13. Walzer, *Exodus*, p. 81.
14. Irving Greenberg, "The Third Great Cycle of Jewish History," *Perspectives* (New York: National Jewish Center for Learning and Leadership, 1981), p. 1.
15. Ibid., p. 8.
16. Ibid., p. 14.
17. Irving Greenberg, "The Ethics of Jewish Power," *Perspectives* (New York: National Jewish Center for Learning and Leadership, 1988), pp. 6–7.
18. Marc Ellis, *Toward a Jewish Theology of Liberation*, second edition (Maryknoll, N.Y.: Orbis Books, 1989), p. 115.
19. Ibid., p. 118.
20. Ibid., p. 120.
21. Gustavo Gutiérrez, *A Theology of Liberation* (Maryknoll, N.Y.: Orbis Books, 1973), p. 161.

22. Naim Stifan Ateek, *Justice and Only Justice* (Maryknoll, N.Y.: Orbis Books, 1989), p. 172.

23. John 1:12–13.

24. Ateek, *Justice*, p. 100.

25. Victorio Araya, *God of the Poor* (Maryknoll, N.Y.: Orbis Books, 1987), p. 69.

26. Ibid., p. 56.

27. Gedaliah Alon, *The Jews in Their Land in the Talmudic Age, Vol. 1*, Gershon Levi, trans. and ed. (Jerusalem: Magnes Press, 1980), pp. 267–70.

28. Louis Finkelstein, *The Pharisees, Vol. 1* (Philadelphia: Jewish Publication Society, 1937), p. 110.

29. Josephus, *Antiquities*, XVIII:1:12–15.

30. John T. Pawlikowski, "Christology as Liberation from Social Sin," *Chicago Studies*, 26, 3 (1987): 290–93.

31. Deane William Ferm, *Third World Liberation Theologies: An Introductory Survey* (Maryknoll, N.Y.: Orbis Books, 1986), p. 42.

32. John Pawlikowski, *Christ in the Light of the Christian Jewish Dialogue* (New York: Paulist Press, 1982), p. 69.

33. Leon Klenicki, "God's Intervening Action," *Christian Jewish Relations*, 21, 1 (1988): 8.

34. Leonardo Boff, *Passion of Christ, Passion of the World: The Facts, Their Interpretations, and Their Meaning Yesterday and Today* (Maryknoll, N.Y.: Orbis Books, 1987), p. 7.

35. Leon Klenicki, June 1989, interview with the author, New York City.

36. Latin American Episcopal Council [CELAM], *The Church in the Present-Day Transformation of Latin America in the Light of the Council. Vol. II: Conclusions* (Bogotá: General Secretariat of CELAM, 1970), p. 49.

37. James H. Cone, "Reflections from the Perspective of U.S. Blacks: Black Theology and Third World Theology," in *Irruption of the Third World: Challenge to Theology*, Virginia Fabella and Sergio Torres, eds. (Maryknoll, N.Y.: Orbis Books, 1983), p. 239.

38. Jon D. Levenson, "Exodus and Liberation," March 1989, manuscript, p. 28.

39. Gutiérrez, *Theology of Liberation*, p. 159.

40. Ibid., p. 158.

41. Ibid., p. 161, reference to Galatians 3:29.

42. George V. Pixley, *On Exodus* (Maryknoll, N.Y.: Orbis Books, 1987), p. 161.

43. Levenson, "Exodus," p. 31.

44. *The Declaration on the Relation of the Church to Non-Christian Religions* (Glen Rock, N.Y.: Vatican II Documents, 1966), pp. 12–14.

45. Harvey Cox, April 1989, interview with author.

46. Harvey Cox, *The Silencing of Leonardo Boff: The Vatican and the Future of World Christianity* (Oak Park, Ill.: Meyer-Stone Books, 1988), p. 154.

47. Juan Luis Segundo, *Liberation of Theology* (Maryknoll, N.Y.: Orbis Books, 1976), p. 74.

48. Araya, *God of the Poor*, p. 53.

49. David Singer, August 1989, in conversation with the author at the American Jewish Committee offices.

50. Rosemary Radford Ruether and Herman J. Ruether, *The Wrath of Jonah* (San Francisco: Harper & Row, 1989), p. 218.

51. Rabbi Greenberg articulated these ideas in an interview in June 1989, in New York and in personal correspondence during August 1989.

52. Ellis, *Jewish Theology*, p. 127.

53. Theodor Herzl, *The Jewish State* (New York: Herzl Press, 1970), p. 80.

54. Ibid., p. 94.

55. Judah Leon Magnes, "Like All the Nations?" in Arthur Hertzberg, ed., *The Zionist Idea* (New York: Atheneum, 1959), p. 447.

56. Vladimir Jabotinsky, "Evidence Submitted to the Palestine Royal Commission," in Hertzberg, *Zionist Idea*, p. 561.

57. This statement was made both by Rabbi Leon Klenicki and by Jacobo Kovodloff, director of Latin American Affairs, the American Jewish Committee, speaking separately to the author.

58. Louis Jacobs, *A Jewish Theology* (West Orange, N.J.: Behrman House, 1973), p. 10.

59. Cox, 1989, interview with author.

PART I

LATIN AMERICAN PERSPECTIVES

1

Liberation Theology

A Political Expression of Biblical Faith

LEONARDO BOFF

THE FUTURE OF THE AMERICAS

What is the future of Latin America? What forces could be of help in the construction of its future? We must ask such questions. It is a matter of hope. No people live without hope. Human societies need utopias in order to bestow meaning upon their struggles for liberation and to find the strength to resist.

Here, in Latin America, there were once major civilizations. Thirty thousand years ago there was already a significant population here. Several socio-economic systems were in force at one time or another, from micro-ethnic groups, through tribal families, all the way to actual empires — power centers with their metropolis ruling over millions of human beings, stratified in different social classes and with sophisticated groups of specialists. With the Aztecs, Mayas, and Incas among others these cultures reached a very advanced degree of social development. They cultivated plants which later became part of the common diet of most of humanity: corn, manioc, potatoes, sweet potatoes, peanuts, peppers, and a vast variety of beans; they also domesticated both cotton and tobacco. Despite their high level of development, however, we should not idealize them. Notwithstanding their advances in communications, processes of urbanization, mathematics, astronomy, the use of the zero at least one thousand years before India (which later on passed it to the Arabs), these high civilizations had their own internal contradictions: a rigid class system of internal domination, slavery, and human sacrifice.

The Iberian invasion, which brought genocide to the native populations, and the spread of European illnesses such as smallpox, measles, grippe, and syphilis all this caused the worst biological hecatomb that we have come to know in history. While Luther was leading the Reformation, and the Council of Trent was organizing the Counter-Reformation (1545-1563), the Spaniards were barbarously decimating the great Meso-American cultures. In fifty years, the population was reduced to barely one ninth. In 1532, according to the accessible data, there were approximately 17 million people in what today are Mexico and Central America. Hardly fifty years later, in 1580, only two million people were still alive in that region. No one protested in the halls of the Council of Trent.

This process still continued, right up to the present. Let me cite an example from Brazil. The Kayapó Indians lived in 1903 on the edge of the Araguaia River, in the state of Goiás, and they were between six and eight thousand. In 1918, because of the white capitalist colonization of that region, only 500 people were left. By 1929 only 27 Kayapós were still alive. Today, this people is completely extinct. Bartolomé de Las Casas, after writing his *Destruction of the Indies*, proclaimed that "The native people . . . have the right to wage a more than just war against us and wipe us from the face of the earth, and this right will assist them up to the day of the Last Judgment."

Because of the Iberian violence against Native Americans, we cannot accept the expression "discovery of the Americas." Instead, we prefer to substitute the more truthful expression "colonizing invasion" — an event which violently subjugated the bodies and crushed the souls of our ancestors. To refer to "conquest" alone assumes a consummated fact, whereas by speaking of "invasion," we give voice to denunciation and stand in solidarity with an ongoing struggle for liberation. Based on this position, we clearly understand why the spokespersons of fifteen Native American Nations rejected, in a letter of July 1986 to the United Nations, the projected celebration of the 500th anniversary of the "discovery" and the "first evangelization" of the Native Americans.

We ask ourselves: How could we celebrate that which meant usurpation, cultural disintegration, ideological subjection, and the death of millions? What would be legitimate instead is a true penitential jubilee, together with a radical reassessment of cultural and pastoral strategies in the direction of a truly liberation option: that of defending and promoting the life and culture of Native Americans. The impact of the invaders traumatized Native American cultures to this day. These could never be rebuilt, culturally or even biologically. Despised, forced to become mestizos, and crushed under oppression, these Native American cultures are today part of the historical bloc of our oppressed peoples, awakening both to evils suffered and to liberation ahead.

The future of Latin America is tied to the future of our Native cultures, recovered, respected, and freed. All other social and moral forces should assume the cause of our Native peoples as their own.

It is in this context that we ask ourselves in what measure both Judaism and Christianity (or better: the Judeo-Christian tradition), so powerful in this continent, could become part of a liberating effort to build for the Americas a human future worthy of its peoples. In this sense, we want to emphasize certain aspects both of liberation theology and of the ecclesial experiences which serve as its foundation, so as to understand our possible contribution to this vast project of creating a future for the Americas.

THE STRUGGLE OF OPPRESSED BELIEVERS

The history of oppression and of the suffering unjustly inflicted on races, peoples, and classes is as old as the historical memory of humanity. Equally long is the history of denial, of resistance, and of attempts at liberation. All oppression and subjection constitute acts of violence which go against the intimate meaning of human life. Therefore one must always expect such violence to be met by protest and rejection, as well as by the desire, never totally destroyed, for liberation. The excellence of human life is basically defined by freedom. Therefore it is not necessary to look for many reasons to justify the search for liberation, that is, that action which makes captive liberty free. It has a value in itself. The story of the ideological use of reason, of philosophy, of religion as instruments of the taming of the oppressed and the justification of the oppressors is a tragic one. Historically, Christianity has been cleverly manipulated by the Western powers in order to subjugate Latin America, colonize Africa and Asia or, for example, to exclude and to persecute the Jews throughout the history of the Christian religion.

What is hidden behind liberation theology? The struggle of the oppressed believers who make their faith a source of mobilization against oppression and for their liberation. In the first place there is a struggle. Struggle here is synonymous with commitment, with organization, with resistance, and with an advance in the direction of freedom. Struggle is the opposite of immobility and resignation. This attitude is perfectly understandable and possesses its own dignity; it is revealed in the many soul-searchings in the post-war period, which were formulated as follows: how can one be human after Auschwitz? How is it possible to believe after Sobibor? The struggle presupposes that this attitude has been transcended. It takes a step forward in the conviction that the historical oppression of great masses of humanity, the centuries-long slavery of the blacks, the subjection of women, the annihilation of the Jews in the Nazi extermination camps, constitute absurdities not totally susceptible to explanation. The struggle presupposes that the historical evil is not there in order to be understood, but to be transcended by a practical alternative which inaugurates the new and thus makes the repetition of the evil either impossible or at least extremely difficult. The struggle is an act of confidence in the human capacity to create relationships of more life and greater justice.

From the 1960s onwards there occurred a great popular mobilization in almost all the Latin American countries. There began to emerge a critical consciousness about the principal causes of poverty and the underdevelopment of the continent. At the heart of this movement there were many Christians who came from the ministry among the workers, the basic education movement (Paulo Freire), the university ministry and other religious activities linked with the poor (the ministry in the shanty-towns, among landless peasants, among indigenous peoples, etc). These Christians began to formulate the following question: how can we consistently be Christians in a world so full of unfortunates? The church, many of them thought, was historically an accomplice in the domination; now it should be an ally in the liberation of the oppressed. They began to read the Bible and the tradition of Christian faith from a perspective which would promote liberation and would denounce the alliance of Christianity with the forces of domination and the maintenance of the present status quo. Assuming the biblical faith, they felt impelled to assume the cause of the oppressed, to make known the iniquity of the oppression which they were suffering and to associate themselves with the movements of social change from the perspective of liberation. The word *development* was avoided and the word *liberation* used. The term development can cover the type of development practiced in capitalist societies: a profoundly unequal development, creating on the one hand great wealth and consumption and on the other misery and hunger. It is impossible to deny the fact that there exists a wealthy center, consisting of the technically and economically advanced countries (situated in the North Atlantic) and an immense periphery which depends on this center and is at the service of the economic, political, and ideological interests of this center, generally made up of the old colonies of the European powers. The relations are not those of interdependence, as if there were equity and proportion in the relations between center and periphery; the relations are those of true dependence in that underdevelopment is seen as the other side of development or as the by-product of the exclusive development operated by the rich countries. The underdeveloped countries are maintained in their underdevelopment, because only with these relations of dependence and oppression can the level of wealth and consumption of the First World societies be guaranteed.

The point of departure for liberation theology is, therefore, the struggle of the oppressed, who make of their faith a special inspiration for social commitment in view of the change in society and, therefore, of liberation and not only the unequal development associated with the development of the central countries. The word liberation means a self-sufficient development, no longer linked to relations of oppression and dependence, but to relations of equity and solidarity. It is concerned with a vast and long historical process which goes beyond the present generation, but which is seen as an imperative of social consciousness and a reply to a fundamental longing of the oppressed peoples.

FAITH AS THE PRACTICE OF JUSTICE

The biblical, Judeo-Christian faith possesses characteristics which open it up to the themes of liberation. Through biblical faith it is affirmed that everything that happens happens beneath the gaze of God; nothing is outside the ambit of God's plan, signified biblically by the Kingdom of God. Faith is always faith in God and in the goodness of God's plan for all creation.

As a God who is alive, this God is extremely sensitive to all those who feel themselves threatened in their lives and cry out for life. Because of this the Bible bears witness always that God is one who hears the cry of the oppressed and takes part in the struggle for liberation (Ex. 3:4-7). God is the God of the Outcry. The faithful know that if they cry out for life, justice, and liberty, God will be listening to them and supporting all that may be done to create more liberty, justice, and life.

Because God is alive and heeding the outcry of the oppressed, God wants justice and abominates all iniquity. It is not the long prayers nor the solemn liturgies which please God, but acts of justice and gestures of solidarity with the weak and those who have fallen on the highway of life (Amos 5:21-7; Is. 58; Jer. 7; Zec. 7).

Finally, God promises a future of life and the reconciliation of all peoples and the coming together of all creation. There will be the Kingdom of God, which is made up of liberty and justice for all, including, as a substratum, the material universe.

Faith in its Christian determination implies the following of the historical Jesus. The practice of Jesus was undeniably liberating. His central message—the Kingdom of God—implies an absolute revolution which must begin with the poor, as they will be the first to receive the Kingdom (Lk. 6:20). In his first public appearance he promises the liberation from concrete oppression (Lk. 4:17-21), afterwards, from the yoke of all legalism (Mt. 5:21f.), always defending the weak against the powerful (Lk. 13:10-17). He considers the act of liberating the hungry, the thirsty, the naked, and the prisoners as that which leads directly to the eternal Kingdom (Mt. 25:31-46).

In all biblical thought true faith cannot exist without the practice of justice and solidarity. St. James, in the New Testament, summed up the tradition well when he said: "faith without works is dead . . . through my works I shall show you my faith" (2:17-18).

Therefore, faith is not manipulated when it is joined with the cause of the oppressed (which is liberation), because the work of faith means justice, liberty, and life. To be liberating is within its own nature.

THE EXODUS AS A PARADIGM OF ALL LIBERATION

In the Latin American reflection of liberation the Exodus, as it is narrated in the Scriptures, occupies a central and paradigmatic place. Already

in 1968 the bishops wrote in the famous Medellín document (which officially inaugurated liberation thematics): "As in ancient times Israel, the
first people, experienced the presence of God who saves, when he freed
them from the oppression of Egypt, so also we, the new people of God,
cannot fail to hear his step which saves when true development takes place.
It is a case, then, for each one and for all, of passing from less human
conditions of life to those which are more human." In the story of the
Exodus we find faith and politics together, the action of historical people
associated with the action of God. We are dealing with a political fact and
at the same time with a theological event. In the Exodus we can see the
two principal moments of any liberation process: liberation-from (from the
oppression of Pharaoh) and liberation-to (entry into the Promised Land).
For the entire Bible, the Exodus constitutes the fulcrum of the people's
faith. On the occasion of the Exodus the people of Israel became a people.
It composed the basic nucleus of the Jewish creed, always recited when the
first-fruits of the earth were presented (Dt. 26:5-9). Even for the New
Testament we understand the Good News of Jesus only if we know the
God of whom Jesus feels he is the son and whom he calls Father. For him
as for the other Jews, this God is "he who brought us out of Egypt, from
the house of slavery."

In the popular mind, the Exodus does not represent a fact from the past.
The people of the Christian communities feel that they are a continuation
of the biblical people. They know that God hears their cries of affliction.
They hope that God will help them in the difficult struggles which they are
undergoing in order to make life secure and to conquer more dignity for
themselves. The Latin American bishops who in the sixteenth century
defended the natives, like those few who denounced black slavery, and the
very native chiefs who rebelled like Tupac Amaru (1780), or Fidel Castro
in his famous self-defense, "History will absolve me" (1953), or the Nicaraguan Sandinista hymn, made and continue to make explicit reference to
the Exodus as the process of liberation from a world of oppression. The
Christian reflection completes this tradition, adding to it what is uniquely
Christian: definitive liberation exists not only when we establish a "land of
milk and honey" but when we transcend death itself and the transfiguration
of the entire universe takes place. The Exodus, then, is the journey of the
whole of humanity and of creation toward the resurrection of all flesh and
the renewal of heaven and earth.

THE POLITICAL RELEVANCE OF THE OPTION FOR THE POOR

In practical terms the essence of liberation theology is concentrated in
the preferential option for the poor. It was first elaborated by the militants
on the ground, then formulated by theology until it was officially adopted
in the documents of the Latin American bishops in Puebla (1979). Today,

through the pronouncements of Pope John Paul II, it has become part of the heritage of modern Christianity.

In Latin America Christianity passes through all the social fabric. Because of this there is a Christianity linked with the interests of the dominant classes, generally a Christianity which is ritualistic, devotional, and spiritualized, but with hardly any ethical sensitivity. There is also a popular Christianity, elaborated by the poor themselves, sometimes alienated in the sense of not helping in the raising of people's consciousness as to the causes of misery (injustice, the rejection of the plan of the Creator), at other times liberating because it realizes that this misery is neither a product of nature nor is it desired by God. The church, as an institution, has lived in Latin America in a pact with the dominant classes. It was part of the reinforcing of the order which maintained slavery and subjugated the workers. It should also be said that there have always been prophets who have denounced this type of collusion as far as religion is concerned. But in spite of that, a religion favoring the powerful predominated.

Through the preferential option for the poor, the church as an institution wishes to shift its center of gravity: from its social place in the midst of the rich it wishes to pass to the social place among the poor, who in fact constitute the great majority of the continent. This option is not exclusive; this is why it is called *preferential*. The church wishes to place all its socio-historical weight, all its moral authority, its resources, behind the cause of the poor. From the poor and the point of view of the poor it wishes to direct itself toward all the other social classes and in this way guarantee the essential catholicity (universality) of the message of Jesus.

In the first place, the option for the poor implies trying to *see* social *reality* and history from the point of view of the poor. They see history as a struggle in order to overcome difficulties, marginalizations, and oppressions of every kind. From the perspective of the poor, capitalist society is evil because it does not allow them a long and decent life; nearly all die before their time, after living in misery. This society must be transformed in order for more social equality to be permitted, as well as more participation and more liberty.

In choosing the option for the poor, the churches assume this vision of the world. Therefore, the church must necessarily be critical of the ruling system; the church is rebellious and liberating, because it postulates the transcending of the present forms of social organization. It is not surprising that these Christians and these churches should be accused by the agents of the status quo of being subversives and revolutionaries. Because of this there exist in Latin America thousands of Christians who are persecuted, imprisoned, tortured and martyred because of their commitment to the preferential option for the poor.

In the second place, the option for the poor implies the assumption of the *cause* of the oppressed. This cause is linked to the fundamental satisfaction of the basic necessities of life: work, shelter, clothing, health, education, and so forth. The poor do not dream of a country which is a great power, dominating others; neither do they wish for Pharaoh-like riches and consumerism. They want those conditions which will allow them a decent life, based on work and political participation.

In the third place, the option for the poor presupposes that the struggles of the people will be assumed. Everything won by the people is at the cost of immense sacrifices, because for them the laws are inadequate, social relationships have deteriorated, security is non-existent and the means are scarce. Everything must be conquered as the result of a struggle. To support the popular organizations, the people's unions, their local associations, their resistance culture, and their popular religion, recognizing the validity of their grassroots communities, their biblical circles, is a present imperative in the option for the poor.

Finally, the option for the poor implies the recognition that the *subject* of liberation is the oppressed themselves, made aware and organized. It cannot be the state, with all its paternalism, or the churches with their aid ethic, or the emotional compassion of certain sectors of the wealthy classes, that will resolve the problems of the poor. It is the poor themselves. The poor person must not be defined as one who simply has nothing, but as one who also possesses creativity, strength of resistance, the ability to survive, the historical force of social change. Only the poor person can liberate another poor person. What the churches and the other social classes can do is to associate themselves with the struggle of the poor. The strategy of transformation and the type of society to be looked for must be defined by the oppressed themselves. It is important to recognize the poor as the subjects of their liberation and of their history. If this does not happen we cannot, in any way, speak of liberation.

As can be deduced from these considerations, the option for the poor possesses undeniable political connotations. It places the churches which take this option seriously in the heart of the social conflict. There the church must, coherently, take her place at the side of the oppressed, sharing in their pain and also in their victories.

A MODEL OF SOCIETY LYING BENEATH THE THEOLOGY OF LIBERATION

It is clear that liberation theology openly opposes capitalism; it sees in it one of the fundamental causes of the situation of the oppressed. But what alternative lies behind the movements which have liberation theology as a reference?

Before anything else we should emphasize the fact that liberation theology has incorporated into its criticism of capitalism many contributions which have come from the Marxist tradition (Marx, Lenin, Gramsci, French academic Marxism, etc.). Because of this, it suffers severe criticism on the part of conservative thinking in the church and from significant sectors of the dominant society. In fact, liberation theology does not assume the Marxist *system*, particularly its philosophical dimension; it incorporates the scientific-analytical aspect which the Marxist tradition developed, particularly in the consideration of the importance of the economic factor in the structuring of society and the manipulation of religion in favor of the legitimization of domination. Therefore, the utilization of Marxism obeys instrumental criteria and it is not used for its own sake. Marx is neither father nor godfather of liberation theology. Inasmuch as he helps to understand the mechanisms of the creation of exploitation and indicates ways of escape from it, he can be said to be a companion in the liberation of the poor.

What would be the alternative to the capitalist system under which the poor suffer so much? Many theologians and pastoral ministers answer: socialism. But we must understand this answer. It is not a case of reproducing actual socialism as it has been in force in Eastern Europe and in so many parts of Asia. Here socialism possesses an analytical and programmatic content; it is that social system in which collective interests possess the hegemony over the interest of private groups in the structure of society. Real socialism means, without doubt, a historical overcoming of capitalism. But in practice it has organized an immense paternalistic state; it does everything, or a great deal, *for* the people, but very little *with* the people and with the critical participation of the people themselves. What is intended, in the theology of liberation, is the construction of a society through the active participation of the greatest possible number of citizens. Not only the party is important, but all the living forces of a people.

Because of this, the majority of theologians avoid the term socialism (because of its political ambiguities) and prefer the words *participatory democracy*. It must transcend the limits of bourgeois representative democracy which in Latin America functions in an elitist and antipopular way, frequently introducing a military dictatorship in order to prevent the advancement of the people and to safeguard the privileges of capital. Participatory democracy is based on the organized people; it can and must have representation, but this is continually controlled by the popular organizations themselves, the true subject of social power. This participatory democracy is not just a project. The seed of it is alive in the popular movements, in the Christian communities on the ground and other movements in which democratic forms of participation are found, together with power sharing.

Participatory democracy depends on the links between these four fundamental factors: (1) the most open *participation* possible, in order to avoid marginalization, and the inclusion of the greatest possible number of people; (2) *equality*, which results from the growing participation of all; (3) respect for *diversity* as an expression of human and social riches, as only thus is uniformity on all levels avoided and pluralism, which is vital for the democratic spirit, permitted; (4) finally, the *communion* which is the search for united human relationships and the opening up to the transcendent as the final end of human destiny and all history.

Participatory democracy represents the alternative to the capitalist social mold which up to now has not succeeded, in any country in the world, in resolving the basic problems of the people in terms of work, shelter, health and education.

CONCLUSION: THE PERMANENT VALUE OF LIBERATION

The theology of liberation is not valid only for those who are oppressed socially and economically. All carry some cross, all suffer from some interior or exterior oppression. For each great oppression its corresponding necessity for liberation has developed. This is how the black theology of liberation grew up in the United States of America, probing into the urgency of the liberation of the blacks in the face of the discrimination suffered by them. African liberation theology particularly stresses that the cultural heritage of the various African people must be preserved, threatened as it is by the invasion of the white Western worldview. There is also a vigorous Asian liberation theology which enters into dialogue with the oriental religions.

Liberation theology represents the first theoretical construction of faith elaborated in the Third World with universal significance. Well-considered, it has furnished the best practical refutation of modern atheism and the Marxist criticism of religion as opium. Religion need not be merely opium. In many parts of the world it constitutes a principle of liberation and an incentive to protest against poverty. The idea of the transformation of society is not exclusive to the Marxists. Many Christians today, in the name of their biblical faith, see a thousand reasons why they should be in favor of a new society in which there would be fewer inequalities and it would be possible to live together in solidarity and with a minimal amount of dignity. Evidently biblical faith is not restricted to this social function. It promises eternal life. But this eternal life is anticipated in the most human and most coherent ways of life, with what we know from the Creator's design. It must always constitute a well of hope for the hopeless of this world and it will betray its nature and its mission if it lends itself to the justification of the present order, which is bad for the great masses of the people. The existence of liberation theology proves that it is possible to keep alive the liberating memory of the Bible and of God's promise to always listen to the cry of the oppressed.

2

Jewish and Christian Liberation Theology

PABLO RICHARD

JEWISH ROOTS OF CHRISTIANITY

Jewish history, according to Irving Greenberg (quoted by Marc H. Ellis in *Toward a Jewish Theology of Liberation*), can be divided into three eras: the biblical, the rabbinical, and the present. The biblical era lasts to the year 70 A.D., when the temple of Jerusalem was destroyed by the Romans. The rabbinical era goes from 70 to the Holocaust of the Jews in Nazi Germany. The third era of the history of the Jewish people begins with the birth of the state of Israel.

Biblical Israel gives birth not only to rabbinical Judaism, but also Christianity. Rabbinism and Christianity are two brothers, sons of the same father: biblical Israel. These two brothers, who always fought among themselves, turned into structures of power and death at a given moment of their history. Christianity became Western Christendom. Rabbinical Judaism became the state of Israel. Western Christendom is responsible for the death of many peoples, and to a large extent, for the Jewish Holocaust. The state of Israel, in turn, is responsible today for the Palestinian holocaust. It is also an accomplice to the death of many Third World peoples.

Christianity and rabbinical Judaism were unfaithful to themselves and broke with their original biblical roots when they became oppressive institutions – Christendom and the state of Israel. Christianity betrayed itself by becoming the religion of the empire, first of the Roman Empire and then of all the empires that dominated the West. Judaism also finally betrayed itself by becoming the oppressor state and the ally of the worst imperialism of all times, North American imperialism.

Both Christianity and Judaism should go back today to their original

identity, rediscover their original biblical roots, and act in solidarity with
their own victims. Christians should have solidarity with the victims of Western Christendom—in a special way with the Jewish people oppressed by
that Christendom. Jews should also have solidarity with the victims of the
state of Israel—in a special way with the Palestinian people oppressed by
that state. The recovery of our basic original biblical identity through the
practice of solidarity is the only possible future, for Judaism as well as
Christianity. This calls for a great humility to recognize our historical errors,
especially for us Christians, the first to betray our original roots by becoming
Christendom and by oppressing the Jewish people up to the Holocaust.

Marc H. Ellis, in his book *Toward a Jewish Theology of Liberation*, and
in his later article, "The Uprising and the Future of the Jewish People,"
rightly insisted on the practice of solidarity, in its political as well as its
ethical and theological implications. Ellis, as a Jew, insists especially—and
with a good deal of courage—on solidarity with the Palestinian people, as
the immediate victims of the state of Israel. As Christians we should also
insist on the practice of solidarity, especially with those who are the immediate victims of Western Christendom: the poor of the Third World. But
we should include among them the oppressed Jewish people, those who
still carry the mark of more than a thousand years of oppression by Christendom, and many Jews who today are oppressed by the state of Israel
itself and who struggle for justice.

Solidarity is not a secondary value in the Hebrew or in the Christian
tradition. The term *hesed* in the Hebrew Bible defines the essence of divine
and human action, and is translated by "mercy," "compassion," "pity." The
corresponding Greek term, *agape*, is best translated today not by "love,"
but rather by "solidarity." The continuity *hesed-agape-solidarity* expresses
therefore the essential ethic of the whole Judeo-Christian tradition. This
ethic was betrayed first by Christianity itself when it became Christendom,
and by Judaism when it became the oppressor and subimperialist state. The
conversion to solidarity is therefore a fundamental demand for both Jews
and Christians. We are Christians or Jews only if we have solidarity. If not,
we are nothing; we have radically lost our ethical-spiritual essence. This
solidarity should obviously begin between Jews and Christians who live
solidarity. The division between Jews who practice *hesed* and Christians
who practice *agape* has radically destroyed both. Even worse, we have made
the God of compassion and solidarity incredible for the world.

When Christianity became Western Christendom, it not only lost its own
identity, it also broke off from its biblical roots sunk deep in the history of
the people of Israel for more than a thousand years. Therefore, as Irving
Greenberg divides the history of the Jewish people into the biblical, rabbinic, and present eras, we Christians could also divide analogically our
history into its biblical-Hebrew era, an era that I would call ecclesiological
(when the Jesus movement became church), and the era of Christendom
(when the church transformed into Christendom: Constantinian, medieval,

modern, or other forms of New Christendom). We should not divide history into rigidly separate eras, because each one always survives in those that come after it: the Jesus movement has always survived throughout the history of the church and Christendom, either openly or underground. But the greater and more destructive danger has been the break between Christianity and its Jewish biblical roots. *We must recover the biblical-Jewish roots of Christianity in order to also recover Christianity as the church of Jesus, denied for centuries by Christendom.*

One of the most ancient Christian heresies was that of Marcion—the heresy that denied the validity of the so-called Old Testament, the heresy that broke the unity of the Old-New Testament. But this heresy is very common today. Many fail to recognize and value the Old Testament, denying thereby the biblical-Jewish roots of Christianity. This leads to a radical deformation of Christianity itself. The Old and the New Testaments are not only two chronological phases, but also two contemporary dimensions dialectically related. St. Augustine's phrase is famous: "The New Testament is latent in the Old and the Old patent in the New." In the Old Testament we have prophecy and institution. Many institutions are surpassed by prophecy; the Old Testament as an institution is surpassed in great measure by the Old Testament as prophecy, but the *prophetic dimension of the Old Testament remains*. Without the Old Testament we could not understand the New Testament, just as we Christians understand the Old Testament from the New.

I think it would be better to avoid the expression "Old Testament" in reference to the collection of biblical books that comprise it, and use the expression "Hebrew Bible." That would avoid undervaluing the Old Testament and give more value to the biblical-Jewish roots of Christianity, as well as improve the dialogue with present-day Judaism. The adjective "old" implies that the Hebrew Bible is no longer valid, something that definitely belongs to the past, something that can be completely surpassed or substituted for by the "new." St. Paul's criticism of the Jewish law is not a criticism of the "Old Testament," but of the transformation of revelation into law—a criticism that can be applied to the New Testament as well as to the Hebrew Bible. The Pauline criticism of the law can apply in the same way to all of Christianity or to any law or secular institution whatsoever.

Liberation theology has recovered in a special way the biblical-Jewish roots of Christianity. It is impossible to understand the New Testament and the whole Christian tradition if we do not begin with the Exodus, the prophets, the Psalms, books like Job, Wisdom, or Daniel. The New Testament, cut off from its biblical-Jewish roots, becomes abstract, ahistorical, easily manipulated. When Christianity loses its biblical-Jewish roots, it simultaneously loses its roots in history and life itself, especially its roots in the popular religious traditions of our time. Many of the spiritualistic heresies of today, arise from reading the New Testament apart from the biblical-Jewish tradition. It is impossible to understand Jesus himself outside that historical Jewish context.

OVERCOMING ANTI-SEMITISM

To the degree that Christianity cut itself off from its biblical-Jewish roots and became Western Christendom, to that same degree Christianity became anti-Semitic or generated anti-Semitic currents. Anti-Semitism, in any case, is basically a Christian creation, even though it comes in secularized versions in the modern era. Already in the Bible itself, especially in the New Testament, there are tendencies that could be interpreted as anti-Semitic. But these tendencies are denied by the *fundamental* biblical message itself, which is profoundly contrary to anti-Semitism.

Anti-Semitism has been without a doubt one of the most violent and destructive doctrines or ideologies in the history of humanity—destructive not only for the Jewish people, but even for Christianity itself. Anti-Semitism is the doctrine or ideology that opposes any realization on this earth of a full corporal life, opposes the total realization of the reign of God in our history, opposes any radical affirmation of hope, of utopia, of freedom. Anti-Semitism tries to destroy the biblical-Jewish roots of Christianity, because it sees in those Jewish roots the origin of all messianic, utopian, and radical movements—movements for a full corporal life and for the full realization of the reign of God on this earth and in this history. Anti-Semitism is essentially antilife, antihope, antireign.

To the degree that liberation theology affirms the extensive action and revelation of God in our history, anti-Semitism also radically opposes liberation theology, as it opposed all movements and liberating theologies in the past. Anticommunism is also a new form of anti-Semitism, to the degree that anti-Semitism interprets the communist movement as a messianic movement that seeks to construct heaven on earth. Anti-Semitism generally opposes all popular movements, because it sees in those movements the realization of the ancient biblical-Jewish utopias of full life and freedom on this earth. In sum, anti-Semitism is identified with antimessianism, and antiutopianism, anticommunism, antipopular liberation. Western Christendom, to the degree that it especially opposes Third World popular movements and liberation theology, is an anticommunist and anti-Semitic Christendom.

It is difficult to understand how Christianity, born of the Jewish liberation tradition of the exodus, of the Jewish prophetic tradition, of the Jewish messianic and apocalyptic tradition, could come to be anti-Semitic; even more, that anti-Semitism be a specifically Christian product. There are no historical facts that would explain the rise of anti-Semitism in primitive Christianity. Jesus seeks to radicalize the prophetic, messianic, and apocalyptic traditions of Israel. Fundamentally, Jesus is assassinated by the Sadducees, in alliance with the Romans, for being a good Jew. Jesus takes his radical critique of the law and the temple from the best of the Jewish prophetic tradition. Thousands of Jews, including Pharisees, are going to accept Jesus as the messiah, prophet, and Son of God, without breaking with Jewish traditions (Acts 21:20). The "Jesus movement" for a long time will be a movement or "sect" within the Judaism of that epoch. Christians, including those from the pagan world, are never going to break with the biblical-Jewish traditions. For a century, the only valid and known sacred scripture will be the Hebrew Bible.

The conflict of Christians is not with the Jewish tradition, but with *a particular interpretation* of the Jewish tradition—specifically the interpretation of the Jews who were in power at that time, specifically the Sadducees, and secondarily the Pharisees. There is no contradiction between Christianity and Judaism. But there is a contradiction between Christianity and Sadduceeism-Pharisaism. Later contradictions will arise not with Jews in general, but with the so-called Judaizers—those Jews who believed in Jesus, but who identified the Christian faith with the fulfillment of the law, especially the law of circumcision. Christians will also oppose nonbelieving Jews. But here also the opposition is not to Jew as such, but to nonbeliever and therefore bad Jew. After the destruction of the temple in the year 70, we no longer have biblical Judaism, but rabbinism, born fundamentally in the academy of Jamnia and in the synagogues of the Diaspora. Christians will be expelled from the synagogues, not as anti-Jews, not for rejecting the biblical tradition, but as heretical Jews, as those who have another interpretation of the biblical-Jewish tradition, one that did not correspond to the interpretation of rabbinical Judaism.

In no way can we understand this contradiction between Christianity and rabbinical Judaism as the historical cause of Christian anti-Semitism. We cannot historically place the rise of anti-Semitism in Jesus, or in the Jesus movement, or in the nascent Christian church. Christianity was not born from the rejection of the biblical-Jewish tradition—the exilic, messianic, prophetic, and apocalyptic traditions. On the contrary, it tried to radicalize those traditions. The critique that Jesus and later Paul made of the law and the temple is a critique that they made as *good* Jews, faithful to the biblical-Jewish tradition that goes back to the faith of Abraham. In no way is their critique an anti-Semitic position.

There are two key arguments for Christian anti-Semitism. (1) The Jews made the realization of the reign of God on earth impossible by killing Jesus. If the Jews had not killed Jesus, we would be living today in the fullness of the reign of God. (2) The Jews should convert before the second coming of Christ. Since the Jews do not convert, they are responsible for the fact that Jesus has not yet come for the second time. If the Jews had converted, we would already be enjoying Christ and his reign on earth. Conclusion: the Jews are responsible for all the evils that we experience. God punishes the Jews so they will convert. Those who do not convert should be killed, so the reign of Christ can come.

How and when did this Christian anti-Semitism arise? How explain that this anti-Semitism has already lasted so many centuries with such violent and destructive force? My fundamental thesis is the following: anti-Semitism does not come from the birth of Christianity, but exactly the opposite, from the birth of a movement to reject Christianity. There is nothing in the history of early Christianity, in the deeds or in the writings, on which the arguments for anti-Semitism mentioned above could be founded. Christianity is born from the biblical-Jewish tradition, especially from its most radical elements, such as the Exodus, messianism, prophecy, and apocalypsis. Christianity is not born in conflict with this tradition. Jesus is killed not by those who believe in this tradition, but precisely by those who reject it. For this reason, to identify the historical birth of Christianity with the anti-Semitic movement would be to affirm the birth of Christianity as an anti-Christian movement.

If that is clear, nevertheless some questions arise. If anti-Semitism is incompatible with the historical rise of Christianity, how explain that historical anti-Semitism had a Christian origin and a Christian existence for centuries? If it is clear that anti-Semitism represents the negation of Christianity, how then explain that an anti-Semitic rereading of Christianity came into being so early and with such force? Would there not be some ambiguities or contradictions in the original historical Christianity that made possible this anti-Semitic rereading of Christianity?

I propose a double task to answer these questions. On the one hand, reinterpret the origins of Christianity in a manner radically contrary to anti-Semitism. On the other hand, reread in a way equally contrary to anti-Semitism all those Christian biblical texts whose ambiguity or possible contradiction gave rise to anti-Semitism, or those Christian texts that have been especially manipulated in an anti-Semitic sense. This task is possible, since it would only be a specific task within the general task already being realized in the spirit of liberation theology.

This general task is the recovery and the rereading of the origins of Christianity from a perspective prior to Christendom. We know that Eusebius of Caesarea wrote in the fourth century a history of the church from a Constantinian perspective to justify the birth of Christendom. The history of Christianity has to be rewritten from a perspective opposite that of Eusebius of Caesarea, from an anti-Christendom perspective. Eduardo Hoornaert has lucidly initiated this work in his book *The Memory of the Christian People* (Orbis Books, 1988). In this context, we need a prophetic-apocalyptic rereading of the origins of Christianity, beginning with its biblical-Jewish roots.

This historical work should be accompanied by serious exegetical work, in which ambiguous texts, or those that can be possibly manipulated in an anti-Semitic sense, can be recovered in their original meaning. This specific exegetical work is also part of a more general exegetical work, also already begun by the exegesis inspired by liberation theology—called a sociological reading of the Bible (especially in the United States), or a liberating or popular reading of the Bible (especially in Latin America). Once this historical and exegetical task is realized, it will become evident that anti-Semitism is a creation much later than the origins of Christianity—a creation, concretely, of Western Christendom.

Moreover, an anti-Semitic rereading of the origins of Christianity was needed to make possible the birth of Western Christendom. Christianity had to be re-created in discontinuity with or in opposition to its biblical-Jewish roots, essentially the exilic, liberation, prophetic, messianic, and apocalyptic traditions. Only an anti-Semitic Christianity could survive in the context of Christendom, a Christianity that will be transformed for centuries into the legitimating ideology of the law and dominating power in the West. We must urgently recover a sense of original Christianity as a "Semitic" current—that is, as a current within the biblical-Jewish movement of a messianic, prophetic and apocalyptic character. The biblical-Jewish roots of Christianity must be recovered and anti-Semitism with a falsely Christian character must be overcome.

CONCLUSION

I have called for the recovery of the biblical-Jewish roots of Christianity and the overcoming of anti-Semitism, especially "Christian" anti-Semitism. We believe that a Jewish liberation theology, like that initially elaborated by Marc H. Ellis, can be an essential help to realize this. Christian and Jewish liberation theology, united in an effective solidarity with the poor and oppressed, is a sign of hope that *it is possible to construct a Christianity beyond Western Christendom, and to reconstitute Judaism beyond the state of Israel.* It is a question of reconstituting the original Christian tradition into a liberated and liberating Christianity; of recovering the Jewish biblical tradition into a liberated and liberating Judaism. This mutual reconstruction should be done in the *practice of solidarity,* in the historical project to liberate all the poor and oppressed. It is important that this process be reinforced by the rise of a Palestinian liberation theology (cf. Naim Stifan Ateek, *Justice, and Only Justice: A Palestinian Theology of Liberation*; Orbis Books, 1989). In a broader context, Muslim, Buddhist, and other liberation theologies are coming into being. The world of the poor is an essentially religious world. It is no surprise that every liberation process also implies the birth of a liberation theology. We have here one of the most powerful signs of hope for the future of humanity, especially for the future of the Third World, where the great religious traditions of the world exist and are being transformed by a sense of liberation.

—*translated by Terrence Cambias*

3

The Holocaust and Liberation

JULIO DE SANTA ANA

Historical processes can surprise the unsuspecting spectator. The observer often tends to think that the lessons of the past have been so well learned that the errors of other eras will never be committed again; and, even more, that others in the future will be spared the harm and the pain of the past. Unfortunately, among the surprises that the course of time brings is the fact that we human beings often do not pass the trials of the novitiate when faced with real life. The struggles for freedom in the past do not mean we can definitely avoid oppression today. In our eyes, then, history appears to be a continuous chain of abuses of power, alternating with freedom and tolerance. This does not mean that history is governed by movements of the pendulum, from despotism to tolerance. As we have always experienced, in history we are again and again caught by surprise. Among the things that startle us is the unexpected, perturbing movement that often changes people from liberators into oppressors.

The change from liberator to oppressor cannot be taken as an interpretive key to understand history in all times and places. This would be to reduce the dynamism of life to an abstract number, cut off from existence, emptied of the substance of reality. It would be to understand the struggles and sorrows of human beings according to geometric figures, as, for example, the figure of the eternal return. By doing this, we forget that historical processes, for those who are involved in them, have a completely original character.

When I state that historical developments involve a recurrent tension between oppression and liberation, in no way do I want to say that all liberators become oppressors. I simply want to recognize concrete situations. The particular and unique elements that manifest that tension has to be perceived in the context of these concrete situations. We must see, in other words, that those who participate in the confusions and surprises of history are always concrete, unique actors.

That is particularly clear when we take into account some of the events and historical developments that have marked our century. The rise and fall of great powers on the stage of history has been noted. The great imperial powers of the beginning of this century have become secondary actors. This pendular movement between oppression and liberation can possibly be seen with greater clarity in the experience of smaller nations and peoples. For example, take the case of the Jewish people. Struggling for their own land at the beginnings of this century, the Jews suffered horrible oppression and persecution. The Holocaust of millions of Jewish men and women under the Nazi regime was the culmination of horrors experienced. When the war against Nazi fascism ended, the United Nations created the state of Israel. The hard struggle for survival began then: from the liberation movement to the constitution of a new state, with innumerable dangers, one of the most important of which was the danger of having their very identity as freedom fighters transformed into reproducers of the image of the oppressors. The creation of the state of Israel was a decision that not only involved Jews. It also had a tremendous impact on the Palestinian people. From the end of the 1940s to the present, the tension between Jews and Palestinians illustrates clearly the tension between oppression and liberation. This tension is difficult to manage. It is at the very center of contemporary history. On several occasions, major conflicts have threatened to break out because of the struggle between Jews and Palestinians.

Israel is certainly not the only case that illustrates the tension between oppression and liberation. These events in the Near East took place simultaneously with the great liberation movement of many African and Asian peoples. It was the irruption of non-Western peoples onto the first page of history. The prelude to all this development was the period before World War II. Nevertheless, when the war ended, the colonial powers were obliged to recognize the right to self-determination and the sovereignty of peoples they had dominated until then. Indonesia freed itself from Holland; India opened the way to the decolonization of the British Empire; Vietnam began its long struggle for independence, first from France and later against the aggression of the United States. In Africa, during the 1950s and the beginning of the 60s, other peoples joined the struggle for national liberation. In Latin America and the Caribbean, Cuba was the first country to manifest the intention to form a society in socialist molds, breaking thereby with a long tradition of dependence and submission of Latin American and Caribbean leaders to Western liberal hegemony. In April 1955 the movement of the "nonaligned nations" was created in Bandung. Freedom and the struggle for autonomy of peoples was a question high on the agenda of "peripheral" peoples. Unfortunately, the processes in use brought new forms of oppression: the liberators of yesterday were transformed into the censors of their own peoples. Challenged by these events, they were moved to organize and fight once again for their liberation.

In other words, the elements that characterize the relations of the state of Israel with the Palestinian people also mark the history of many nations of Africa, Asia, Latin America, the Caribbean, and the Pacific. This ever-recurring tension between oppression and liberation calls for reflection. Human thought cannot ignore the social and economic conditions in which it takes shape. Moreover, thought is tightly bound to these conditions. Sociological reflection, the attempts to understand human beings in their life situation, the grid that helps weave together philosophical and theological thought—all demonstrate how related they are to the experience of being oppressed and struggling for liberation. André Neher, for example, one of the most brilliant French Jewish thinkers, reflecting on the situation of Judaism in the context of Western civilization, takes into account not only Auschwitz and Hiroshima, but also the confrontation between North and South. For Neher the "iron curtain" is not between East and West, but between peoples who have manifested a clear materialist vocation, be it under capitalism or socialism, and other communities who witness to cultural traditions thousands of years old, where the religious factor has been preponderant. In this way, Neher is situated, when he reflects on "Jewish existence" in the context of the great confrontations of our century.[1] This same tendency is found all over. In the West the problem is posed in terms of the aberrations manifested by the (bad) use of power.[2] The search of black peoples to reaffirm their identity was made in the context of the tension created by the confrontation between oppression and liberation.[3] In Asia, let "Minjung theology"[4] stand as one of the many expressions of what I am saying here. In Latin America and the Caribbean, we see the irruption of new anthropological thought, as well as the birth and growth of the "theology of liberation."[5] In all these cases, in spite of the different contexts in which these tendencies of contemporary reflection took shape, the ultimate reference is always the oppression-liberation tension.

The theme is vast. I do not intend to treat it here. In this essay I am interested in reflecting on the common elements as well as the differences (in some cases, contradictions) between two expressions of these intellectual tendencies of our time: Jewish theology of the Holocaust and Latin American liberation theology. The first came into being among the people of the Torah; the other among those who emphasize the tremendous importance of hope, nourished by "promise." Both are biblical theologies. Nevertheless, they are not parallel.[6] They have points in common, from which they challenge one another.

THE RADICAL REFERENCE TO THE POOR

Through the ups and downs of their history, the Jewish people have always looked to the fulfillment of their law to assert the meaning and the particular orientation of their lives, their specific vocation. The law's fundamental objective is to respect the *other*, because one gives praise to God by recognizing the *other*. *Others* lose dignity when they have to humiliate themselves to survive. This is the misfortune of the *poor*, whom the Old Testament books consider as oppressed. Because of this, we can say that in the Torah poverty is considered an evil, as a painful fact that has its roots in oppressive, dependent relationships. These relationships lead to the false exaltation of the powerful (false because it does not respond to God's will, to God's truth) and to the humiliation of the helpless. From this perspective, poverty, oppression, and misery are considered as abnormalities. The person who seeks to be faithful to God finds in the Torah orientations to correct these evils. The command to help the poor, the widow, the orphan, the foreigner, and the slave are very clear in the law (cf. Exod. 21:1-11; 22:20-23).

These precepts characterized the social life of Israel, as a federation of tribes sharing the fruit of their labor to the satisfaction of all. Injustice and oppression were established to the degree that some groups instituted mechanisms of domination that allowed them to take advantage of the surplus produced by the farmers. This was the disgrace of the monarchy (cf. 1 Sam. 8:10-18). From then on, poverty grew in Jewish society.

The prophetic movement defended the poor, in a spirit of fidelity to the covenant established by Yahweh with the Jewish people. This is very clear among the prophets of the eighth century B.C.E. Seeing how the poor were afflicted by the crisis of their time, leaving them often almost totally destitute, they denounced the forms of oppression that allowed for a certain type of economic growth favorable above all to those who already had money. Amos, for example, is going to denounce suffocating taxes and interest (Amos 4:1; 5:11-12), fraudulent commerce (8:4-5), the enslavement of those who could not pay their debts (2:6), unjust judges (5:12), and other abuses. Micah, for his part, denounced the hoarding of lands (Mic. 2:1-3). Isaiah upbraided the corruption of the authorities who made harmful decrees favoring the powerful and crushing the rights of the weak (Isa. 10:1-2; 32:7). All this is against the will of Yahweh.

For this reason, the prophets in the Old Testament corroborate the ideology that makes the king the protector of the poor (Isa. 11:4), which Jeremiah understood to be fulfilled in the reign of King Josiah (Jer. 22:15-16). In the book of Deuteronomy, the Torah establishes that "there should be no poor" in Israel if the precepts of the law are kept (Deut. 15:4). For this reason, to be *just*, to do justice (*tsedaká*), consists in helping the poor, doing whatever is necessary so they can overcome their condition of poverty. Justice, therefore, comes from below, since poverty is not misfortune, the consequence of destiny, but the fruit of the irresponsibility of those who work injustice and oppress their neighbor. The struggle of the prophets consisted in demanding faithfulness to the Torah. To do that, above all their word had to be concrete, and therefore also faithful to reality. The prophets had the audacity to refuse to be manipulated when interpreting the reality in which they lived. They denounced falsehood, as well as the practice of the oppressors who took advantage of the misappropriation of wealth. At the same time, the prophets announced that the justice of God is inexorably fulfilled throughout history.

The poor, then, are God's favorites. A certain form of spirituality developed in ancient Israel from this fact, especially when the exiles returned from Babylonia. The "poor of Yahweh" are those who through their painful experience came to know the divine strength of the poor and oppressed, and who sought out the Lord. This spirituality is clearly expressed in some of the Psalms (9:11; 34:11). The attitude toward God consists in abandoning self to God's will and accepting God's plans, as expressed in the Torah (Ps. 10:14; 34:9; 37:40). There is no reason to fear the powerful of this world; God must be feared (Ps. 25:12-14; 34:8-10). The poor are integral, right, and just when they observe the commandments of the Lord (Ps. 34:16, 20, 22; 37:17-18). Because of this, the "poor of Yahweh" are God's friends. God's enemy is the proud person who tries to oppress the poor and the weak, to take advantage of them. By doing so the proud person ignores the presence and the challenge of the *other*.

The prophets raise their voice, as "word of God," against the proud. Their word is based not on some abstract demand, but on the inalienable rights of the poor. The prophets speak from the perspective and position of the poor. André Neher is correct when he affirms that "from one end to another, the history of Judaism is shaped by the dynamism of the poor, the miserable, the persecuted. They built the Biblical City, constructed the synagogue, constituted the Jewish people."[7] It is a question, fundamentally, of a struggle against all that alienates human beings. The goal is the joy of being alive, the liberation of the sabbath, when the person is reconstituted not only as a worker, but also as someone who reflects on and celebrates the God who gives life to be lived, to be happy.

This liberation calls for overcoming every type of bitterness. And the need to overcome bitterness leads to a consideration of the emphasis given by a good deal of contemporary Jewish theology to the Holocaust. Some theology of the Holocaust is still marked by bitterness, in reaction to that horrible moment when the Jewish people suffered such cruelty. The problem of bitter people is that they do not liberate themselves from the force that struck out against their person, their being. The bitter have injected this force into their own life. They have not liberated themselves from this force. For this reason, they use it against others. Some strains of the theology of the Holocaust try to theologically legitimate bitterness, by trying to justify an aggressive power for the state of Israel, which in one form or another shows itself to be oppressive and unjust to the Palestinian people. The worst evil that oppressors can commit is to pour out their own guilt feelings—which they inevitably have in virtue of their practice of oppression—onto the oppressed person. The oppressed, then, takes over the same orientation in life as the oppressor. If the oppressor sought to dominate the other, using any means possible, the oppressed almost mechanically and unconsciously repeats the attitude of the dominator. In other words, the oppressed do not transcend their situation.

For this reason, Marc Ellis is correct when he says the theology of the Holocaust should be replaced by a *theology of solidarity*, through which the Jewish people would give a full expression to their universal vocation. The emphasis should be on the extension of the faith, and not on its exclusivity. This practice of solidarity begins with those who are closest. The *other*, the Palestinian, calls for recognition, dialogue, life with open relationships. This is what is written in the Torah. More than a Jewish liberation theology, it is a challenge to the Jewish people to develop a profound practice of liberation. Solidarity, beginning with the Palestinians, will be the indelible proof that bitterness has been overcome. And, let us not forget, the Holocaust was a horrifying expression of bitterness—something that should never be repeated, not even by the Jews.

When we turn to Latin America and the Caribbean, we have to recognize that we find many reasons that also call for bitterness. It is a situation characterized by the "suffering of the innocent,"[8] as Gustavo Gutiérrez so well expressed it. The innocent peoples of Latin America endure violence, injustice, pillage, which brings suffering and pain. They are peoples comprised by the poor:

In effect, they are victims. We must repeat it, because by speaking so much of the poor, the commitment to them, their human and Christian values, their evangelizing potential, we run the risk of forgetting all that is inhuman and antievangelical in the situation of the poor. The real poverty that the immense majority of human beings live, and not that idealized poverty that at times we fabricate for pastoral, theological, and spiritual necessities.[9]

Liberation theology in Latin America and the Caribbean was not born by chance. Liberation theology is a faith reflection that begins with the questions of the poor—the immense majority of the Latin American and Caribbean peoples; questions raised by the injustice they experience, questions related to the need to survive amid hunger, misery, sickness, and death. Due to the impact of Christian faith on the life of the poor, these reflections arise naturally in theology.

The poor no longer accept their situation. They have begun to fight—according to their possibilities—for something more than survival. They seek to live more abundantly. To live with justice. With freedom. The struggle for liberation unites them. In the face of authoritarian oppression, of exploitation imposed by unjust economic powers, the poor of Latin America assert themselves as an emancipating force. Of course it is not an exclusively Christian movement. Communities of faith, united with other popular sectors, participate in the journey of their peoples toward a better future. Christians and non-Christians join in this liberating practice through many different social movements. This has led to new forms of being church, especially grassroots ecclesial communities. One of the fundamental elements that characterize these communities is the practice of solidarity. This calls for a break with the existing order. The innocent suffer where solidarity is lacking. It is impossible to try to be in solidarity with the poor in a system dominated by egoistical passions and the rationality that gives priority to self-interest. This unjust system is to be found in the marketplace, where appetites bring people to compete with one another. Solidarity demands that we turn our backs on this world.

A dead end, a new road, advances and retreats—the whole movement is under the call and action of the Spirit that asks us to think, feel, and live with Christ (cf. Phil. 2:5) in the now of our lives. This demand is perceived with particular urgency by Christians committed in one way or another to the liberation of the poor in Latin America:

> The option for the poor and their liberation is responsible in Latin America for a time marked by a great effort of solidarity. A solidarity that comes precisely as an expression of Christian love. A solidarity rooted moreover in the cultural traditions of the indigenous people of this subcontinent.[10]

From what was said above, we can see with greater clarity the proximity between the theology of Jewish existence, so marked by the tragedy of the Holocaust, and Latin American liberation theology. Both have the poor as a constant reference point. Max Weber, in the chapters dedicated to the sociology of religion in his *Economics and Society*, attacks the "religions of the poor" as expressions of bitter peoples. Their messianism comes from this bitterness, according to the German professor. Weber, in this case,[11] although referring to Nietzsche, does not see that Nietzsche's typology of the characteristics of a bitter person points in reality more to the bourgeois than to the truly oppressed.[12] A good deal of bitterness was needed for the Aryan bourgeoisie to bring the Jewish people to the Holocaust. The suffering that the international bourgeoisie imposes on the peoples of the Third World, especially those of Africa, Latin America, and the Caribbean is also proof of much bitterness.

A very important point in common between the theology of the Holocaust and the theology of liberation is the recognition that an oppressor exists. The oppressor talks of freedom, but imposes laws in an authoritarian manner. The only freedom that the oppressor recognizes in practice is the freedom of the market. The market, with its providential and "invisible hand," eliminates all suffering. Unfortunately, this is not true. The proof is there: Auschwitz and Treblinka are part of bourgeois bad conscience; they cannot be erased. In the same manner, the deterioration of the quality of life, the gradual death of African, Latin American, Pacific, and other Third World peoples—remember also, along these lines, what is happening in the Amazon jungle, so pillaged by the demands of the market—all are things that reveal bourgeois bad conscience. And when we speak of bad conscience, we are speaking of guilt.

The trick of oppressors has been to give that bad conscience to the oppressed. For example, indebted peoples are judged for not being able to pay even the interest on their external debt. There is no mercy for them. They must pay, even if this means less life for them. The guilt of the irresponsible creditor is passed on to the powerless debtor. In these cases, the temptation to bitterness is very strong.

That temptation must be overcome. To do so, both Jewish theology and liberation theology have sufficient resources. Yahweh, the God of Jesus, is the God of life, the God who listens to the cry of the oppressed. God is certainly a warrior God. But God's combat is for justice for the poor. God's struggle is a liberating struggle. And in this sense, both Jewish and Latin American liberation theology affirm that the agents of God's liberation rise from the people. Liberation presupposes, as we have already seen, the refusal to remain captive to a situation characterized by bitterness. Liberation transcends sorrow and anger, confirming solidarity. This also means affirming life as a gift of God. This affirmation corresponds to the existence of the poor. Those who oppress and corrupt the poor pour out their bitterness on indigent men and women. The poor, on the other hand, are strengthened through the practice of solidarity.

THE REFERENCE TO THE EXODUS

I cannot allude to the tension between oppression and liberation in history without referring to the biblical story of the Exodus. Throughout the development of Jewish thought, both in ancient Israel and after the tremendous catastrophes of 70 and 135 A.D., liberation is understood primarily through the grand gesture of the liberation of the Hebrew people from the yoke of the Egyptian pharaoh. Previous liberations (Abraham's departure from his homeland, Jacob's wrestling with the angel) are also seen through and from the liberation of the Exodus. The return from the exile is also understood through the same prism. Every time a profound crisis touches the people of Israel, in one way or another they refer to the Exodus.

It happened that way, for example, in the catastrophes of 70 and 135. The fall of the temple confirmed the Diaspora. The promise of the return to the homeland motivated the dispersed people. More profoundly still, the defeat of Bar Cochba in 135 was interpreted as an indication of the almost total abandonment in which the people found themselves. Dispersed and defeated, they felt the challenge to rebuild. This reconstruction can only be understood correctly in terms of liberation—in other words, in relation to the Exodus. The exodus-liberation theme showed the rabbis how to restore the meaning of the Covenant (*berit*) in the consciousness of the people of Israel.

The liberation from Egypt is linked to the promise of the Holy Land. For Jewish consciousness, there is no exodus without a Palestine. This was especially evident when, at the beginning of this century, the movement to "return to the homeland" held its fourth congress in Basel (August 1903). The congress discussed the possibility of accepting the British government's offer of the territory of Uganda in East Africa, since the immediate return en masse to Palestine was not feasible. Herzl wanted to accept. The Russian delegates, on the other hand, fought all night long to reject the offer. Zionism's importance for the Jewish spirit can be seen in this incident. Jewish identity, for much of Israel's consciousness, is linked to being in Palestine.

This felling—better yet, this realization—was expressed not only through the Zionist movement during the greater part of this century, but also especially through the subversive struggle for the independence of the state of Israel. We must also not forget the important fact that progressive sectors of the Palestinian people gave valiant support to the combat of the Zionist movement. So it went that in April 1948 the state of Israel was finally recognized. Unfortunately a new problem arose: the situation of the Palestinians. From that time on, the Exodus ceased to be a challenge and became a memory—a motive of celebration, which for many does not have sufficient force to liberate Zionist ideology from its exclusiveness. Of course, the Exodus continues to be the central reference of Israel's faith—the nucleus of its religious profession and of its "credo" (Deut. 26:4-9)—which the Jews celebrate each year at the time of the Passover. The Exodus, for Jewish consciousness, is the beginning of the Covenant (Exod. 19-24) that makes Israel the people of God.

Surprisingly, when the Exodus event was read some thirty years ago from the perspective of the poor of Latin America and the Caribbean, it began to be perceived as a contemporary reality. I have already mentioned the underdevelopment, oppression, and poverty that characterizes the Latin American masses. When they reread the account of the flight of the Hebrew people from Egypt, the words have a special ring. They state that the experience of the people led by Moses can be repeated—obviously in different terms—in the history of the Latin American and Caribbean people. Without claiming that what happened then is the same as what these people experience now, the story of the Exodus is read as an inspiration for life, as nourishment for hope. The Second General Conference of the Roman Catholic Episcopacy in Latin America (Medellín 1968) expressed this feeling clearly:

Just as Israel of old, the first People [of God], felt the saving presence of God when He delivered them from the oppression of Egypt by the passage through the sea and led them to the promised land, so we also, the new People of God, cannot cease to feel his saving passage in view of true development, which is the passage for each and all from conditions of life that are less human, to those that are more human.[13]

The exodus theme appears regularly in the reflections of Latin American liberation theologians. The reference to this biblical story nourishes the faith of the poor. The Exodus can be considered as a hermeneutical key for the life situation that the poor of Latin American and the Caribbean experience today. These peoples interpret history with a "messianic criterion."[14] History is the setting for a permanent struggle for liberation. God is not only present in the past; God opens the ways to the future. Even more, the promise of God and human desires for a more just, free, and fraternal world converge in the future. The practice of liberation mediates the passage through today's suffering to that new reality.

Precisely at this point the theology of liberation challenges the theology of the Holocaust. As we said above, the state of Israel came into being after the tragic experience of Nazi persecution and Jewish genocide in concentration camps. This took place in the threatening context of the beginning of the "cold war" and the hostility of most of the Arab world. The state of Israel was clearly vulnerable and weak. Israel feared that the Holocaust could be repeated in a different way. This fear and the bitterness from the sufferings at the hands of fascist Nazism were extremely important factors that led Israel to adopt the behavior of its former oppressors. It based this policy on a "realistic" view of the world. *Si vis pacem, para bellum* — if you want peace, prepare for war. As we know, it is difficult to only prepare for war. Very often the will for national security leads to aggression.

The state of Israel has proven that many times: oppression of the Palestinian masses; three open wars with Egypt, in two of which Israel was the party directly responsible for beginning hostilities; a permanent arms race in the region, certainly one of the most militarized on the planet; development of armed nuclear capacity; active arms producer; open support for regimes that define themselves as reactionary and conservative, such as South Africa and various Latin American military dictatorships. . . . And if that were not enough, an openly repressive attitude toward the Palestinian uprising that began in December 1987. A will that denies dialogue, negotiation. In sum, a practice that takes a definite stance against the liberation of many oppressed peoples.

Most of the so-called "theology of the Holocaust" defends (granted, with nuances) that reactionary attitude of the state of Israel. It tries to legitimate it theologically. Here I have to ask a question: Is this position only an institutional, political expression (what could be considered a "reason of state"), or does it involve something much deeper, which affects the very life of the Jewish people, their own spiritual roots? Or, to put the question in another way: Is it a tactical position of the state of Israel, or does it come from a profound determination of the Jewish people, which results in an almost uncontrollable orientation?

Latin American liberation theology raises a question at this time. How to keep alive the spirit of the Exodus? How to be faithful to a vocation to freedom and justice? How to avoid that God's call be transformed into a motive of hubris, and, on the contrary, how to maintain that vocation through a constant practice of gift, of solidarity?

This is not the first time in history that the Jewish people give signs of putting aside the spirit of the Exodus. Already in the time of ancient Israel, when the monarchy arose from needs considered inevitable (the need to organize better the defense and administration of public life, among other things), little by little the spirit of liberation and justice was put aside. I already spoke of the prophets' reaction to such an attitude. When we observe the life of the Jewish people today, we have the impression that an important sector is repeating that same experience, while other sectors struggle to keep alive fidelity to the vocation of Israel. Those who opt to legitimate aggressiveness and authoritarian attitudes in some way express a spirit that represents the priesthood, producer of symbolic goods that nourished the nationalist and exclusivist aspirations of postexilic Judaism. They demand, as representatives of the priestly spirit, that there be sacrifice. Obviously the offering does not include the Jews. Today, unfortunately, the Palestinians are sacrificed.

This attitude provokes serious doubts for many Christians who, conscious of the gravity of the crimes committed against the Jews by the Nazi fascist forces and their allies, adopted a posture of unlimited support for the state of Israel and the Jewish people. Now, seeing the spiritual rigidity and the dogmatic authoritarianism that characterize the Zionist movement, they ask with anguish if they should continue their support for Israel. And many, consciously, in fidelity to the spirit of the Exodus, understand that they can no longer continue upholding a policy that, in the time of Moses, was the same as taking the Pharaoh's side against the Hebrew slaves. They ask themselves about the spiritual attitude of the Jewish people: Will they be able to put aside priestly arrogance? Will Judaism be able to free itself from the power of the temple? Liberation theology insists that the abolition of priestly power was the project of Jesus, who was also Jewish.

CONCLUDING REFLECTIONS

The Jewish people cannot be assimilated to the Zionist movement. Without denying the importance of this movement, we must keep in mind that in the Israel of today there are sectors that have a position about the Palestinian question diametrically opposed to that of the leaders of the state of Israel and the intellectuals who try to legitimate the leaders' position, either theologically or politically. We must recognize the importance of the state of Israel. The lesson learned by the Jewish people through history is clear: they have to have a state. The problem is what kind of state.

A state is a series of institutions that allow for the development of a nation according to its fundamental specificity and vocation. It brings together institutions that administer *laws* that help social development. Are the *laws* of Israel today consonant with the Torah? What is the relationship between the *reign of God* and the state of Israel? When the laws that allow the administration of the state to become a yoke (first for others; then for the very citizens of the state), then it is far from the *reign of God*. On the other hand, when those laws have as their foundation a spiritual discipline that tries to express the imperatives of the law (*halaká*) in always renewed forms, the presence of the *reign of God* in history is undeniable. That means that if the *halaká* responds faithfully to the meaning of the Torah, liberation (not only of Israel, but of *all the peoples of the Earth*) must be assured.

It seems to me that this strongly challenges the Jewish people of today. Not only the citizens of the state of Israel, but also the whole multitude of the Jewish Diaspora. To sum up, that is the great challenge that Latin American liberation theology presents to Jewish theology today. It undoubtedly implies the demand to transcend the theology of the Holocaust, or a theology that is fundamentally priestly. It is a request that theology also free itself, that it cease to be exclusive, and that it live in a practical way the extension of the gift — a life that not only nourishes itself from memory, but also, and especially, nourishes itself from promise. The promise of God that opens the future to *all* human beings.

— translated by Terrence Cambias

NOTES

1. André Neher, *L'existence juive* (Paris: Seuil, 1962), pp. 274-77.

2. See from the vast bibliography on this theme: Max Horkheimer and Theodore Adorno, *Dialectic of Enlightenment* (New York: Seabury Press, 1972), pp. 168-298. Also the works of Michel Foucault. On the complicity of bourgeois philosophy with Naxism, see the recent polemic on Heidegger, opened by the book of Pierre Bourdieu, *L'Ontologie Politique de Martin Heidegger* (Paris: Minuit, 1988).

3. Walter Rodney, *How Europe Underdeveloped Africa* (Dar-es-Salam: Tanzania Publishing House, 1972). Also, Leonard Barnes, *African Renaissance* (London: Victor Gellanez, 1971).

4. CTC-CCA, *Minjung Theology. People as Subjects of History* (Maryknoll, New York: Orbis Books, 1983).

5. Gustavo Gutiérrez, *A Theology of Liberation* (Maryknoll, N.Y.: Orbis Books, rev. ed. 1988).

6. André Neher, *L'existence juive*, p. 15. On the importance of hope in Latin American liberation theology, cf. Rubem Alves, *Theology of Human Hope* (Washington, D.C.: Corpus Books, 1969).

7. Neher, *L'existence juive*, p. 265.

8. Gustavo Gutiérrez, *On Job* (Maryknoll, N.Y.: Orbis Books, 1987).

9. Gustavo Gutiérrez, *We Drink from Our Own Wells* (Maryknoll, N.Y.: Orbis Books, 1984).

10. Ibid., p. 145.

11. Max Weber, *Economia y Sociedad* (Mexico City: Ed. F.C.E., 1969), vol. 1, pp. 394-98.

12. Frederich Nietzsche, *Genealogia de la Moral*, in *Obras Completas de Federico Nietzsche*, Tomo VIII (Buenos Aires: Ed. Agular, 1954). Gilles Deleuze, in his *Nietzsche y la Filosofía* (Barcelona: Ed. Anagrama, 1971), systematizes the thought of Nietzsche on the "type of bitterness," characterized by: (a) the incapacity to admire, respect, love; (b) passivity; (c) search for usefulness; (d) its tendency to impute errors, distribute responsibilities of blame, to be an eternal accuser. This allows for the perception that the *pariah peoples*, embittered, be found especially among the bourgeoisie.

13. General Secretariat of CELAM, *The Church in the Present-Day Transformation of Latin America in the Light of the Council. Vol. 2, Conclusions* (Bogotá: 1968), Introduction, p. 49.

14. Rubem Alves, *Da Esperança* (Campinas, Brazil: Ed. Papirus, 1987), p. 143.

PART II

A Jewish Theology
of Liberation?

4

Breaking the Chains of Necessity

An Approach to Jewish Liberation Theology

MICHAEL LERNER

Judaism emerged as the first historical liberation movement by challenging the necessity and the inevitability of systems of oppression.

Whenever one group of human beings dominates and exploits another, the exploiters find it necessary to justify this arrangement. That need stems from the fact that human beings recognize in each other a commonality and feel a natural attraction and desire to connect, sympathize, and care for each other. This is not to suppose that there was once a golden age in the past when everyone lived in peace and harmony. It is easy to imagine that in the distant past the competition for scarce resources may have set people into conflict with each other. But before the development of agriculture those struggles were necessarily brief encounters—not necessarily enshrined in the organization of the communities within which most people lived. It is only with the development of class societies based on agriculture that we have a systematic enslavement of one group to another—and the corresponding necessity of the enslavers to find a way to explain to themselves why this arrangement is legitimate.

Justifications for oppression, then, emerge first as a self-justification, and not as a means of convincing the oppressed that they ought to like or accept their oppression. Until the last three hundred years (and then it was different only in Western capitalist societies), the primary mechanism that perpetuated class societies was the ability of rulers to effectively mobilize violence to subdue those who might challenge the existing order. Yet even where violence was the primary means, we should not underestimate the importance of ideology and mass psychology in perpetuating a system of oppression. Though we have no reason to believe that ruling classes ever self-consciously set out to create belief systems that would justify their class rule, throughout history they have tended to be attracted to religious, philosophical, and ideological systems, manifested in art, dance, drama, literature, and religious ritual, that have explained why the way the world was currently ordered was the appropriate way.

The most common form these ideological approaches have taken throughout human history is the following: the actual class divisions in society are described as "natural" — that is, built into the structure of necessity, having the same power and inevitability as nature itself. Just as the sun rises and sets, fall and winter follow spring and summer, the moon goes through a fixed cycle, so also . . . and then this is followed by some description of some aspect of society that simply cannot be changed or challenged ("everyone has a king," or "certain types of people are destined to reign and others destined to do agricultural labor," or "there will always be inequalities or injustices in society," or "there will always be rich and poor," or "people are naturally aggressive or acquisitive").

There may well have been other slave revolts or other forms of rebellion against oppression before the Exodus of Jews from Egypt. Moreover, there are many historians today who doubt the historical accuracy of the story as told in the Torah. Both points are irrelevant to the fundamental point being made here, because it was not the actuality of the rebellion and the Exodus that made Judaism the historical source of revolutionary thought. Rather, it was the telling of the story — the creation of a worldview, embodied in Torah and relived every week in the Sabbath as a minicelebration of the Exodus — that from its inception infuriated ruling classes, earned the Jewish people the enmity of every class society, and kept the Jewish people on the forefront of revolutionary innovation and social change. It is in insistence on telling the story, and making that story the center of Jewish religious life, that the Jewish people became the living embodiment of a perpetual challenge to the ideologies that claimed that existing forms of oppression are inevitable and built into the structure of necessity.

To put it most starkly: sometime between 1400 and 400 B.C. the Jewish people got the message or developed the insight that human reality was fundamentally different from natural reality as understood in the ancient world. Human beings and the societies in which they live do not follow an inevitable pattern of nature. Rather, human beings are free to create a very different reality — a reality in accord with the fundamental insight that all human beings deserve a certain level of dignity, respect, and love. That which has been in the past need not be that which shall be in the future: the future is radically open to new possibilities.

Moreover, not only are human beings free to create that kind of life for themselves — they have an obligation to do so. Life as a slave is fundamentally in conflict with the nature of human beings. So class society is wrong, a violation of our human essence. The Exodus, far from being one possible choice among many equally valuable possibilities, was the only humanly justifiable choice.

The notion that we are free to break the chains of the past, and that it is our obligation to do so, is the essence of the revolutionary message of Judaism. The domination of the past over the present is not inevitable, and through our own activity we can make things different—this is the spirit of Torah that has permeated Jewish consciousness, and makes Marx and Freud true descendants of the Jewish tradition, not merely its biological offspring.

Nowhere is this spirit more clearly embodied than in the injunctions of Torah about how to live once the Jewish people enter into their new (promised) land. Here was a people beaten down and subdued through four hundred years of slavery. They had learned the ways of thought and approaches to reality of Egypt. Everything we know about psychology teaches us to expect that human beings will pass on to the next generation much of the oppressive life patterns and ways of viewing themselves and the world that have been impressed upon their consciousness when they were in a weak and vulnerable position.

ON NOT RE-CREATING A WORLD OF OPPRESSION

It is a commonplace to expect that the battered child will grow up into a batterer, that the oppressed, if given the freedom to do so, will become oppressors—not because human beings are innately evil, but because the way we have learned to be when we are weak and vulnerable is the way we continue to be when we are no longer so weak and vulnerable, and possibly also because, as Freud would have it, in acting out under conditions of relative power the patterns we experienced when we were totally powerless, we seek to gain some degree of mastery and control over that which was imposed upon us. Yet, counter to this expectation, the Torah screams out to the Jews a very different message: When you go into your land, do not re-create Egypt, *do not re-create a world of oppression.* You do not have to do so. Your own experience as people who were oppressed may create a psychological tendency to become oppressors, but it simultaneously has created another possibility: the possibility of remembering your experience, and using that as a basis for identifying with the oppressed, and not re-creating that oppression for others in the present. No injunction is stated more frequently in Torah than one or another version of the following: When you come into your land, do not oppress the *ger*—remember that you were a *ger* in the land of Egypt. *Ger* here means exactly what the Jews were in the land of Egypt—a powerless minority, a group that is not in the position to control its own destiny.

That the Jewish people today are explicitly violating this injunction by their treatment of the Palestinians will come as no shock to anyone familiar with human history. A people that has just emerged from the gas chambers and crematoria of Europe—having learned the lesson of their inability to rely on other human beings for the most minimal support—might not be expected to immediately overcome the scars of two thousand years of Christian and Islamic oppression. Those of us within the Jewish tradition criticize the current policies of the state of Israel—but even we have some compassion for the people of Israel, even as we condemn their policies as self-destructive, paranoid, and immoral. Yet we are not surprised that the Jewish people itself is not the living embodiment of the principles of Torah. Torah's revolutionary message of the possibility of human liberation is still only a message of possibility. To actualize this possibility in human life is yet another and more difficult step. Indeed, the Torah itself is a record of a people both attempting to actualize that possibility and falling away from it. It contains both moments of magnificent transcendence in which the revolutionary possibilities become manifest and explicit to an entire people, and many more moments, perhaps even the majority of moments, when the Jewish people are in active flight from these same realizations, seeking instead to build various golden calves and reject the monumentally scary notion of their own freedom and their moral responsibility to build a world based on that freedom.

The story of the Jewish people throughout their history as a vanguard people, a people that brings the world the message of liberation, is necessarily the story of a people that is itself in internal conflict and struggle. It is not the story of a people that has magically transcended the past and thus able to serve as a living example of the truths it projects to the world. Rather, it is the example of a people that is in constant struggle with God, willing both to proclaim God's truth and constantly running away from that truth, and often unable to describe to itself which of these two it is doing. Yet the struggles of this people are the struggles that anyone or any group must go through if they are interested in advancing the cause of human liberation. Anyone or any group that seeks liberation may have its moments of transcendence, to be sure: moments in which they are able to break with the thought patterns and emotions of the past and to glimpse the possibilities of human beings actualizing their freedom in a world based on mutual respect and caring. Yet, even at such moments, everyone participating in such insights will hear the message as refracted through his or her own psychological and conceptual framework, a framework inevitably tainted by the history of oppression. And as we move from those moments of transcendence, it is inevitable that we will confront, just as the people of Israel did historically, a tendency to retreat and hide, to build our own institutions and practices that protect us from staying in touch with the scary and yet joyful possibilities of human liberation. That every liberation movement will inevitably go through this kind of an oscillation between closeness to God and retreat is my contention. By studying the way that this happens in Torah, and in the subsequent history of the Jewish people's relation to Torah, we learn how this process works, and at the same time we get tools that can help us recognize our own process of retreat and self-deception.

Because it is easiest to recognize this process in the story of Moses and the Exodus, for the moment we shall ignore the book of Genesis and pick up the story when Moses discovers God—God as the embodiment of a vision of the possibility of human freedom and transcendence, a God who breaks the laws of nature by both burning a bush and not having that bush consumed. There is a principle or force in the world that transcends nature, that is not reducible to its laws, and that will not accept the inevitability of human oppression and humanly created suffering. As God puts it to Moses in the first communication, "I have deeply seen the suffering of my people who are in Egypt, I have heard their outcry because of their taskmasters, because I understand their pain. . . . I shall send you to Pharaoh and you shall free my people" (Exod. 3:7-10).

A GOD WHO INTERVENES IN HUMAN HISTORY

But who is this God? Moses understands the need of human beings for a concrete reality. Slaves live day to day, they need something tangible and real that they can put their fingers on if they are to believe it is real. They do not want abstract principles or theories of possibility. At the very least, they need to know how to identify this God. So, Moses asks, "When I come to the Israelites and say to them 'The God of your fathers has sent me to you' and they ask me, 'What is his name' what shall I say to them?" And God said to Moses, "*Ehyeh Asher Ehyeh* . . . Ehyeh sent me to you." Literally, I shall be who I shall be; tell them that "I shall be" sent you. That is, this is the God whose very name is the possibility of transcendence, freedom , and self-determination. The past does not inevitably rule—there is a new possibility in the universe, a force for freedom, a force that is based on the notion that the human world is not fixed and inevitable, that it can be changed in accord with our ability to hear the cry of the oppressed, and to join with a God who understands the pain and suffering of the oppressed and insists that it be stopped. This is not a God who passively submits to the pain and sheds tears in heaven but remains absent on earth. Rather, this is a God who has intervened in human history, through the agency of the Jewish people, to give the message to the world that this pain and suffering can and ought to be ended.

If we hear this message as it was intended, we also understand the universal message and revolutionary impact of Torah. For, as Genesis proclaims very clearly, all human beings, not just the Jews, are created in the image of this God. Everyone of us participates in this possibility of freedom, transcendence, and identification with the oppressed, which are the essence of this God.

Just as we all participate in the possibility of freedom, so we all participate in the actual retreats from God that characterized the Jewish people's response. On the one hand, having been empowered by the experience of the Exodus, once the Jewish people are confronted by God they respond by saying that "All that God has spoken we shall do" (Exod. 19:8). On the other hand, as soon as they experience the revelation in its full force, they are so overwhelmed by it that they immediately back away, asking Moses to be the intermediary: "You speak to us," they said to Moses, "and we will obey; but let not God speak to us, lest we die" (Exod. 20:16).

Much of the rest of the text reflects the fear of transcendence, and the reappearance of the ways of Egypt. At the very moment that Moses is on Mt. Sinai receiving the rest of the teachings, the people are down below building a golden calf. They are unable to take the leap to total freedom or to relate to a God who is the principle of freedom and moral responsibility. God, the story goes, is faced with a people that cannot accept its freedom, and inevitably begins to repeat the patterns of oppression. They want a God who can be seen and touched; they want something related to the world of empirical reality, that which actually and already exists. From this point forward, the Torah that is received is a Torah that is a divine compromise between what it would be really like for human beings to act on the reality of being created in the divine image, on the one hand, and the limitations on human possibilities generated by the psychological, cultural, and intellectual inheritance of having grown up in a world of oppression. It is only in terms of this compromise that God introduces the ritual sacrifices, the construction of the sanctuary, and eventually even the possibility of Jews having a king.

For those who find it difficult to hear God-language, we can tell this story in their language as well (after all, according to the midrash the Torah was given in seventy different languages so all could understand it, and our task is partly to rediscover all those different languages). It goes like this: the Torah is the account of a moment in human history when the possibility and moral necessity of human liberation first became evident to an entire people. Yet that insight entered into the consciousness of a people that was itself the historical product of a world of oppression. Inevitably, then, the way that it received that insight, the language in which it was clothed (God-language), and the attempts to embody it in ongoing institutions (the laws of Torah) were themselves all influenced by the psychological and ideological limitations of the people who were its recipients.

Whether we tell this story from within the religious paradigm or from without, we are still stuck with a frightening task: to distinguish those parts of the story that are essentially true to the original liberatory insight or divine revelation from those parts that are the product of the historical distortions inevitably introduced by the limitations of those who received the insight or revelation. To raise the issue in this way is to recognize that any reading of Torah will essentially be *our* reading—not *the way it was written* but rather our own particular interpretation, just as every other is a particular interpretation.

It would not matter if we were to believe that every letter of Torah was directly given by God—the long history of commentary on Torah proves beyond a reasonable doubt that what the Torah means requires interpretation, and often elicits opposite interpretations. It is always specific human beings in specific circumstances that *do* the interpretations, and these human beings have always been (just as we are today) limited and distorted by the ideological, psychological, and spiritual framework with which they approach Torah. As the Jewish prayer book says, "This is the Torah which Moses placed before the children of Israel, by the mouth of God by the hand of Moses"—that is, although transmitted through divine revelation, it is necessarily received by a particular and limited human being.

There is no escape, then, from the task of reading the Torah, and the historical interpretations of Torah, with a critical eye. We must always distinguish between moments when we can hear the voice of God and moments in which we hear the reappearance of the psychological and intellectual residues of the world of oppression.

"But why bother?" you might ask. "After all, if every reading is simply *our* reading, and we are forced back on our judgments and intuitions and insights, then why not just stick with those insights that are available to us anyway without the text?" These are two reasons to bother. (1) It turns out historically to be a matter of fact that the grappling with this tradition and its texts has the consequence of producing a greater openness to the transcendent insights that are found within them. In theological language, the revelation of God is to be found there, and even though it may be refracted through human receivers, it is there nevertheless in a way that it may not be equally available in other texts or places. (2) The process of learning how to distinguish between the voice of God and the historical distortions introduced by those who heard that voice is a process that is absolutely necessary for us—because it gives us some sensitivity to the ways that we may ourselves be distorting our own perceptions in our own times.

For example, we can watch how God tells Moses, "Go to the people and warn them to stay pure today and tomorrow. Let them wash their clothes. Let them be ready for the third day; for on the third day the Lord will come down in the sight of all the people on Mount Sinai" (Exod. 19:10-11). And Moses then changes the message in verses 14 and 15: "Moses came down from the mountain to the people and warned the people to stay pure, and they washed their clothes. And he said to the people, 'Be ready for the third day; do not go near a woman.'" For Moses, the divine injunction to stay pure translates into not going near a woman, because Moses has been brought up in a sexist social order that makes that equation, *even if God does not.* It should be no surprise to us, then, if at a later point Moses begins to hear God's voice differentiating in responsibility and obligations between men and women.

What should surprise us at any given moment in approaching the texts and the history of their interpretations is not what parts seem totally consistent with the existing social order, but what parts seem to transcend and confront the existing norms, ideals, and social realities, articulating something different, unique, transcendent. When we hear principles of justice, commandments not to oppress the powerless, injunctions to love our neighbors, ideas about the redistribution of wealth (for example, as embodied in the Jubilee Year), and limits on the rights of property, all of which seem to be ahead of their own times (and in some cases, ahead of our times as well), then we have reason to pay attention to those parts and ask if we are hearing at such moments instances of the voice of God being most clearly communicated.

On the other hand, when we read parts of the text that seem to reflect the values and norms of the society from which the writings emerged (for example, the sexism of various passages, or the commandments concerning the conquest of the land of Canaan), we need not be shy in saying that we do not hear in those passages the voice of God speaking, but rather only the distorted perceptions of the people. Nor is this some suddenly modernist sensibility that comes to do its selective readings. Any serious student of midrash and the interpretive literature from the Talmud on through the great *mefarshim* (medieval commentators) will testify that the interpretations often reflect an implied embarrassment at the plain meaning of the words, and an attempt to uncover different meanings more consistent with the interpreters' understanding of what could make the text consistent with their own intuitions about what is truly divine.

THE VOICE OF GOD AND THE VOICE OF SELF-DECEPTION

Yet the very process of struggling to differentiate between the voice of God and the voice of the self-deceptions of the age must also be applied to our own insights. For example, in the past several hundred years in capitalist society the dominant paradigm of human life has asserted that each of us is radically distinct from each other and to be valued for the ways that we are different, independent, and self-determining; that we are the possessor of a set of individual rights that are the most important thing about us; that we enter into human relationships as independent contractors whose highest obligation is always to look out for our own interests; and that since we are free to make whatever we will out of our lives and our world, we have no one but ourselves to blame if we do not achieve individual satisfaction and fulfillment in our lives. These truths, embodied in the self-justificatory structure of every institution in the capitalist world, become so "self-evident" that it is almost impossible to *not* allow them to shape our encounters with the divine and with the holy texts. And yet . . . precisely our practice at questioning the "self-evident" truths of earlier ages gives us the facility to recognize the moments in which the ideological framework of our own society may be shaping our own intuitive apparatus.

In this process we may begin to imagine new possibilities — for example, allowing ourselves to imagine what it might be like to live in a world in which we began to value ourselves and fellow human beings not only for what was unique about each of us, but also for what we had in common (our shared "species being" or human essence or set of human capacities and possibilities); a world in which we saw ourselves not as set apart from each other but as fundamentally and necessarily linked so that our own survival and destiny was seen as inextricably linked to the future of the human race; a world in which the need to be (healthily and not as a result of societal or familial coercion) lovingly connected to people was given primacy over the needs to "make it" or "determine our own individual destiny" and in which the healthy human being was not judged to be the one who had achieved individual ego autonomy but the one who had learned how to allow herself or himself to be most fully loving. The dialectical interaction with the self-deceptions of earlier ages as reflected in the texts helps build this kind of ability to imagine and fight for alternatives in the present reality.

It is precisely this tradition of struggling to extract the divine voice from the texts that allows Israel to live up to its name as the one who wrestles or struggles with God. Yet it is always us, very limited human beings, who must engage in that enterprise. We are the embodiment of the collective experience of the human race, refracted through the specific experience of our nation, our people, and our own family, and shaped by the ideologies and forms of life that are available to us as we grow to maturity in a specific class society. Just as every generation before us has had its limitations when it approaches the divine, so do we. Just as every other generation has been overwhelmed by the spirit of the divine, run away from it, asked others to interpret it for us, so have we. We need only look at the way we abandoned the spirit of the 1960s to know how frightening it is to come face to face with the possibility that the world could be radically remade. We need only watch how quickly so many from our generation have sought interpreters for God's word, rather than trusting their own ability to listen, for us to understand some part of the experience of the generation of Israel in the desert.

The limitations are real, but they too can become a false god, an idol to be worshiped, part of a "reality" that we must adjust to rather than transcend. How easy it is to fall into an intellectual or cultural relativism in which there is nothing to do but to deconstruct the texts, endlessly trapped in inaction as we contemplate the various perspectives, any of which might be true (or none, because on this perspective there is nothing but perspectives). The revolutionary message of the Torah is just as relevant here as it was for the Jews leaving Egypt. That message is: the world can be radically transformed, that which has been need not be all that which can be. We as human beings are partners with the divine in re-creating the world, and we are commanded to do so in accord with God's plan for a world based on love, justice, and compassion.

My rabbi and teacher Abraham Joshua Heschel said that the dominant motto for contemporary society might well be: "Suspect Your Neighbor as Yourself." Self-doubting and other-doubting are easy to come by in this society. What is much harder is a grounded compassion, the ability to see how we have acquired our limitations through the combined impact of childhood pains and social conditioning interacting with our own choices as we came to perceive them, the ability to see that our limitations (and those of others around us as well) are not a reflection of inherent evil or stupidity but rather a reflection of the impact of the accumulated experiences of the human race as reflected through our particular family, and hence the ability to see that we are not to blame for those limitations. To the extent that we can overcome the self-blaming that inevitably leads to other blaming, we become empowered to have the courage to listen to the voice of God, manifested in the world and refracted through the texts. It is such moments of courage that lead us to hear the liberator message of Torah.

I believe that when we hear that voice as it was heard by Moses and the children of Israel, we hear a voice that tells us that the history of oppression is a history that can be broken, that the cycles of pain can be ended, that psychological and social conditioning can be transcended and changed.

5

A Jewish Journey through Nicaragua

Phyllis B. Taylor

Jalapa, Nicaragua. The year was 1983. I was sitting in a small room in a building in Jalapa, the first delegate of Witness for Peace listening to three mothers describe the life and death of their sons. This town and its immediate surroundings had been fought over by the Nicaraguan Army and the Contras, for it is surrounded on three sides by Honduras and especially vulnerable. As the first mother began to talk about her son, she started off with her voice strong and sure, until she came to the day that she heard he had been killed. At that point she began to cry. The second mother then began to talk about her son, again in a strong, commanding voice, until she came to the day she heard her son had been killed. She, too, began to cry and so did I. The third mother then began and she too began to cry. I went to the first mother. We held each other and tried to comfort each other through the wordless act of the embrace. She was a mother whose child had been killed by the support and money of my own government; and I, a Jew, who had just learned a deeply humbling lesson in love and forgiveness.

Let me go back, though, and explain how I ended up in Jalapa and in other towns in Nicaragua. It becomes a story that had its beginnings even before I was born. One of my grandfathers emigrated to the United States as a teenager, after being chased into a house by a cossack on horseback intending to kill him. My other grandparents came to Brooklyn, New York, to escape the hatred and persecution of Jews in eastern Europe at the turn of the century. It was in Brooklyn that my parents were born, met, and married in 1940. I was born in 1941 during the Holocaust, on the other side of the ocean.

Just before my brother's birth in 1944, my parents moved to a town on Long Island. The original inhabitants to the town did not want Jews in their neighborhood. They set up their own schools and social clubs, and I grew up hearing about signs saying, "No dogs and Jews allowed." I also grew up during the revelations about the destruction of European Jewry and the birth of the state of Israel. In our home we were never allowed to have anything German. I grew up hating Germans and hating Arabs, since both groups seemed determined to destroy us. I used to stand in front of a mirror and think that I would be dead if it were not for the fact that my grandparents fled eastern Europe because of anti-Semitism.

My tears while holding the grieving mother in Jalapa were for her and her family, and for myself as well. How could she forgive me, a U.S. citizen whose government was responsible for her suffering because of our foreign policy? What enabled her to distinguish between individual German citizens and the Nazi government policy or between Palestinians and the policy of some leaders who wanted to destroy Israel? The mother's hugs and tears taught me an invaluable and transforming lesson about love and forgiveness, one that carries over into all parts of my life today.

As a child my world had been ripped open by the stories of Auschwitz and Bergen-Belson, of the Warsaw uprising, and Anne Frank. I remember storming into the bathroom one day while my mother relaxed in a warm tub. With all the arrogance of a young teenager, I demanded to know how she and others could have been silent when millions of men, women, and children were being killed. How could she have had children, bought a home, and gone on with life when all this was happening to our people? With great arrogance, I determined that I would try not to be silent when killings and other forms of injustice were occurring in my own country and around the world.

In my high school and college years I found myself doing a great deal of questioning. Did God exist? If yes, how could God have let the Holocaust happen? How could "good" people have been so silent? Was I now one of the "good" people or did I need to speak up whenever I saw or heard about injustice? These questions led me into the civil rights movement, the movement to stop the war in southeast Asia, and the movement to foster human rights throughout the world. That led me to marrying another civil rights worker whose values were the same as mine but who was a Christian, the first "real Christian" I had ever met. Through the years we ended up having a homemade son, adopting an Amerasian daughter from Korea, and raising and educating a foster daughter from El Salvador. And we found ourselves increasingly concerned about the wars in Central America.

In the midst of working for justice in the U.S.A. and peace in other areas of the world, I went back to school to become a registered nurse with the hope of going to Central America for various periods of time. Right after finishing nursing school, I met two former church workers who together had spent almost thirty years in Guatemala. I shared with them my dream of going to Central America as a nurse. They asked me if I really cared about the people of Central America. If I did, they said, then I ought to work in the United States, since it was our own government's policies that were causing so many of the hardships in the Central American countries. That was not what I wanted to hear, but I realized they were right.

In 1983 my life took another twist that brought me to Central America not in the traditional role of a nurse but as someone trying to change U.S. foreign policy so that my nursing skills would not be so necessary. In April 1983, Gail Pharis, an excellent organizer who had lived in Nicaragua, took thirty people to Managua and Jalapa for five days. They arrived for their day in Jalapa right after a Contra attack. The buildings were still burning and a woman wandered around in a daze after members of her family had been hurt. Some of the survivors said that they felt they could relax, because they did not think the Contras would attack while there were U.S. citizens in the village.

Gail returned to the U.S.A. with those words burning inside her. She helped organize a trip in July of one hundred fifty U.S. citizens who would go to Nicaragua for five days. Dick, my husband, went. He, and a small group of others, felt that somehow other U.S. citizens needed to go to Nicaragua to see the reality of the country for themselves, since our press would not report what they had seen and heard. On the twentieth anniversary of the famous March on Washington that Dr. Martin Luther King, Jr., so eloquently spoke at, telling the nation and the world that he had a dream, a group of people from the earlier peace trip and a few others gathered in the basement of a house in Washington before and after the march. An invitation to go to Nicaragua as Witnesses for Peace (WFP) came from some members of the Nicaraguan church community, and we wanted to respond.

As one who was at that founding meeting in Washington and then our first formal meeting in Philadelphia in October 1983, I had to make sure that I felt comfortable with the basic WFP principles that we adopted. There were fundamental issues I needed to address. One was a belief in God and the other was commitment to nonviolence.

Our statement of purpose reads:

To develop an ever-broadening, prayerful, biblically-based community of United States citizens who stand with the Nicaraguan people by acting in continuous nonviolent resistance to U.S. overt or covert intervention in their country. To mobilize public opinion and help change U.S. foreign policy to one that fosters justice, peace, and friendship. To welcome others in this endeavor who vary in spiritual approach but are with us in purpose.

For many, many years the knowledge of Auschwitz made me feel that there was no God. I progressed in my spiritual journey by deciding that if there were a God, I would hate a God who would have allowed the Holocaust to happen. I finally decided that God did exist and that Auschwitz could happen only because people were quiet. I found the analogy that the power of God is like the potential for light in a room. What is needed is for someone to turn on the light for the room to go from darkness to light. I decided that one of the reasons that the Holocaust could happen was that individuals did not open themselves to the power and mandate of God to make a more just and loving world. They did not turn on that spiritual switch. Micah chapter 6 had always moved me. In it the prophet says, "What does the Lord require of thee but to do justice, love mercy, and walk humbly with your God?" I felt that WFP was one way to make that directive more visible in Nicaragua and in my own country.

Having grown up with a great deal of hatred and the knowledge that never again should we be silent and led to slaughter, and yet having been deeply moved by the commitment to nonviolence I lived with in the civil rights movement, I had to come to terms with the concept of nonviolence. While participating in freedom rides, I went through nonviolent training. I saw nonviolence as a tactic. However, through the years as a civil rights worker and peace worker, I met many, many people who viewed nonviolence not just as a tactic but as a principle for living. Dick, my husband and companion in these journeys, was the first pacifist I ever met. I eventually found myself viewing nonviolence as a way of life and saw it as the dynamic, active entity that I believe it is. I personally adopted the definition that Dick developed: "Nonviolence is a powerful, active way of working for human liberation that firmly and clearly resists and refuses to cooperate with evil and injustice, while attempting to show goodwill toward all and taking suffering on itself rather than inflicting suffering or violence on others." Lack of violence is only one-fifth of the definition. Resistance to evil and injustice, withdrawal of cooperation from those who perpetuate evil and injustice, the showing of goodwill toward friends and opponents, and the willingness to suffer, if necessary, are all part of that definition. I again felt that WFP was a way to translate that definition of nonviolence into reality.

Given my good feelings about WFP and my desire not to be silent when injustice is manifest, I volunteered to coordinate the first short-term WFP delegation. Our destination was Jalapa. Besides the deeply moving experience I had with the mothers whose sons had been killed, and the revelation about forgiveness, for me as a Jewish woman, one other experience in Jalapa touched me greatly.

We had had a difficult time getting to Jalapa because of Contra activity in the area. Now we found that Contra activity was delaying our scheduled departure. As we waited for the old school bus we rented from a Baptist school to get word that the fighting had stopped and it was relatively safe for us to go, a young mother carrying her baby began to talk to us. The mother asked one of the WFP women to set her hair while we waited. I played with little Ricardo. At one point, the mother asked if I would take Ricardo back to the U.S.A. When we asked her whether she wouldn't miss the baby, her eyes filled with tears as she shook her head "yes." She said she would come for him after the war was over, but she wanted to make sure nothing happened to him until then. It reminded me with a tearing at my heart of the Jewish mothers who tried to pass their children on to others so they would not be killed. Having my own children and a grandchild, I can hardly imagine the desperation that mothers in wars must feel and the sacrifices they are willing to make to enable their children to live. We explained to her that we could not take Ricardo with us but we would return to the U.S.A. and do everything in our power to stop the war so he could grow up.

The second and third delegations I coordinated and took down to Nicaragua were Jewish WFP delegations. I kept hearing charges from President Reagan that Nicaragua practiced systemic anti-Semitism. That was not my impression, but it was something that the Jewish delegations wanted to check out. While in Managua we had the chance to talk to Rolland Najlis and his daughter Michelle, a Nicaraguan poet; Herty Lewitis, the minister of tourism; Carlos Alleman Ocampo, a Mid-East specialist with the Nicaraguan ministry of the exterior; and many others. We also said kaddish, the mourner's prayer, at the Jewish cemetery in Managua. It was very moving to stand among the neatly marked stones, engraved in Spanish and Hebrew, and to pray that ancient prayer:

May God's great name be praised and sanctified in the world! May your rule be established in our lifetime and the lifetime of the House of Israel. God's great name is blessed and praised far beyond all blessings and praises we could ever say in the world. May there be a great peace from heaven and life for us and all Israel. May the One who makes peace in the high places, make peace for us and all Israel!

I was aware that we were repeating the same words that the Jewish families whose loved ones were buried in Managua said. They were also said in Jewish homes, synagogues, and concentration camps around the world.

We also went to the former synagogue, which is now painted with children's murals. We had heard reports that the cemetery and synagogue had been defaced with swastikas, but we saw no evidence of that. The Najlis family and others with whom we spoke, including people from La Prensa, the opposition newspaper, and even U.S. embassy people, all told us that there had been random acts of anti-Semitism, but nothing that was systematic or would indicate government sanction. We reflected that Jewish synagogues and cemeteries are defaced in the United States, but none of us would say that the U.S. government is fundamentally anti-Semitic.

During the first Jewish delegation in December 1984, we celebrated Hanukkah, lighting the first night's candles in El Bloque, Somotillo, in the northwest section of the country. People in Somotillo had no idea what Jews were, so it was a challenge and treat to interpret who we were and to share with them the festival of lights, the festival of Hanukkah. One of the members of the delegation wrote the following, which another member translated for the Nicaraguan children who joined us:

Tonight is the first night of Hanukkah, the festival celebrating our liberation as Jews, from the Greek tyrant Antiochus. It is especially moving to celebrate it here tonight in Nicaragua, in El Bloque, in solidarity with the Nicaraguan people.

The word *Hanukkah* means dedication, as in the dedication of a new home. Two thousand years ago, under Greek oppression, even the practice of our religion was forbidden. Finally, Matityahou the priest, and his sons led by Judas Maccabeus—our Sandino—led the people in a guerilla struggle to liberate our land, and to worship again in the way of our ancestors.

On this night, two thousand years ago, the temple in Jerusalem was liberated. In joy, the people rushed to purify the temple, and to dedicate it once again in the service of the Creator.

But they found only enough purified oil to light the temple Menorah for one day. Eagerly, they sanctified the Menorah and lit it anyway. And miraculously, the Menorah remained lit for eight days, until new oil could be purified. This is the miracle that we celebrate tonight, and for eight nights in all. We do not celebrate the military victory—although it was necessary—but that the Creator responded to our desire to worship and kept the Menorah lit.

This is also the Nicaraguan miracle—not the military victory that came with the overthrow of Somoza—but that the revolution still lives. It is the strength and faith of the people that we celebrate—as in the days of our ancestors, so is it now—that between the practice of our religion, and the freedom of the people, there is no contradiction and must be no contradiction.

"Tonight we light the first candle of Hanukkah, dedicating the first candle to our unity, and the intertwining of our histories."

The second Jewish delegation, in 1987, was in the Wiwili area, a town that had been bombed by the Honduran air force and then mortared by the Contras. We were there during the celebration of Purim, the festival of Esther. It also seemed very appropriate to be celebrating this holiday, which focuses on the resistance of Mordecai to the oppressive prime minister, Haman, and the nonviolent civil disobedience of his niece, Esther, to save the Jewish people from destruction. Once again, there was a sense of the entwining of our lives with the people of Nicaragua.

This was especially strong for me during the night we spent at a small resettlement village north of Wiwili. We arrived by dugout canoe, since there were no roads. The afternoon was spent hearing the heartrending stories of what the war has meant to the people of this village. They talked of killings and kidnappings. As night fell, we sat on the ground, waiting to get some instructions on where we should hang our hammocks. As it got darker, the stars got more beautiful. To minimize our sense of vulnerability sitting out in this remote village with no lights and with sounds of guns periodically firing, we began to sing. We sang in English and the curious villagers who were around us began to sing in Spanish. There was a mixing of Spanish, English, and Hebrew song during this amazing day of warm welcomes, the sharing of sorrow, the joy of a spontaneous dance in one of the few completed community buildings, the tying up of hammocks in the elementary school building, which was made of a roof and poles to support it but no sides, and finally falling into a tentative sleep accompanied by the sounds of nature and the periodic crying of babies.

The evening before we left Wiwili, some villagers asked us to worship with them. We gathered in an open field and the service began. Our delegation had many fluent Hebrew speakers but not many Spanish ones, so following the words was difficult but not the spirit of the people. During the passion of the peace, which was a new and moving experience for us, I felt my eyes filling with tears. I began to wonder, when would I get back and, if I did return, who would be absent because of the war? As the service ended we moved down the road singing, "Shalom Charerim," which ends with the words, "til we meet again, til we meet again, shalom, shalom."

We were witnesses to try to bring shalom, peace, to the Nicaraguan people and to our own. I realized that in my own life there is a unity. It began for me when I first learned about the Holocaust and what can happen when people do not listen and witness. It continues for me in the journeys to Nicaragua. One of the members of the first Jewish delegation said well much of what I was feeling when she wrote the following. I read it as we stood in front of the U.S. Embassy in Managua:

We are the first Jewish Witness for Peace delegation. We follow twenty or so delegations that have come from the United States in witness to the war in Nicaragua. Our Judaism brings us to this place because our tradition asks us to speak out against injustice. We as a people are committed to "Tikkun Olam," the just restitution and repair of the world. We, as a people through our tradition, have accepted the responsibility of preserving the world in our laws, our text, and mostly in our hearts. . . .

Forty years ago Jews learned just how unjust people can be against each other. We learned that there is no torture beyond comprehension, no reason when the path to destruction is set and that the lesson from the Holocaust, "Never Again" has a special meaning. We know, as a people, that there is no such thing as an injustice happening to someone else; it happens to us all. We have come to Nicaragua to witness the war, and we will return to our families, communities, and elected representatives and tell them what we have seen. We read this statement as a proud, strong people whose own history demands that we be present today in solidarity with the Nicaraguan people.

The journey continues. As I again prepare to return to Nicaragua with another Jewish delegation, the words of the Shema are engraved in my mind. Upon my heart and on my lips is the song that says, "Til we meet again, til we meet again, shalom ... peace ... shalom ... peace."

6

God's Joke

The Land Twice Promised

ARTHUR WASKOW

To be clear about the ground from which I speak: I am passionately committed to wrestling God as part of the people named *Yisrael* — "Israel, God wrestler." I feel connected with Martin Buber, Franz Rosenzweig, and Abraham Joshua Heschel (their memories be for a blessing) in the last generation, and I look forward with eagerness and trepidation to the coming of Messiah — be it speedily and in our own day!

When I address the issue of the land of Israel, my first thoughts are:

- That God promised that land to the people of Israel on permanent and irrevocable but intermittent loan (for ownership of that land, like all land, belongs to God);
- That Israel's actual possession of the land is intermittent because possession depends on how well Israel follows the commands of Torah to hallow the earth and human society;
- That every intervening exile from the land, caused by Israel's failure, no matter how long the exile, will be followed by another chance;
- That the contemporary state of Israel is the form the Jewish people's continuing experiment in fulfilling Torah in the land takes, in our generation;
- That Israel is commanded also to live among the nations, in order to learn from them and teach them; in order through dialogue-in-action to renew its own, and their, holiness and creativity.

These are my first thoughts. I hold them out of my own reading of God's Word as revealed in Torah, in the human heart, and in history. These first thoughts are not unusual in the Jewish community, though the last one among them is not universally accepted.

73

My second thought is held by far fewer people in the Jewish community. It is that in some sense God has also promised a relationship with the same land—not necessarily the same kind of relationship—to another people: the children of Ishmael, in our generation represented by the Palestinian people.

This too I learn from God's word revealed in Torah, in the human heart, and in history.

Why would God promise the same land twice to two different peoples, even if the two promises are somewhat different? And why do I say there are two promises, anyway?

First, in the text of Torah (Genesis 16-17 and 20-21), the story of the struggle between Abraham's two wives and their two sons—Hagar and Ishmael, Sarah and Isaac—is the paradigm of the struggle between Jews and Arabs. According to the traditions of both peoples, the Jews are descendants, physically and spiritually, of Abraham, Sarah, and Isaac; the Arabs, physically and since the coming of Islam spiritually as well, are the descendants of Abraham, Hagar, and Ishmael.

In that story, Sarah insists that for Isaac's good, Ishmael and Hagar must leave the family. Abraham is troubled, but God upholds Sarah's wishes. God promises to continue the covenant of Abraham through Isaac; but God also promises to make of Ishmael a great nation, and prophesies of Ishmael that he will be a wild jackass of a man (that is, a nomad); he will lift up his fist against everyone and all will lift their fists against him; and finally "he will dwell face to face with all his brothers" (Genesis 16:12).

Somehow, somewhen, Isaac and Ishmael must learn to live in each other's presence after being separated. Indeed, in their own lifetimes the two are reconciled when Abraham dies (Genesis 25). They meet again at their father's grave in Hebron, the grave that in our generation has become the scene of bitter contention, of raised fists and worse, between their descendants.

Why were the brothers separated? And how can they be reconciled?

To understand, we need to remember that Isaac was the younger of two sons and that over and over in the Book of Genesis, there can be peace between brothers only after a period of enmity and strife. So it was with Jacob and Esau and with Joseph and his older brothers.

To understand, we also need to know that Isaac's name (in Hebrew *YiTzChaK*) means "Laughing Boy." And we have to know that when Sarah accuses Ishmael of "making sport with" or "mocking" Isaac (Genesis 21:9), the word she uses is *MiTzaCheyK*—from the same root of "laughing." *The same root.* Ishmael is acting out the "laughter" that is at the root of Isaac's soul, and this playful aspect of Ishmael is playing havoc with Isaac's identity.

How can we experience this agony, this havoc? Take a mirror. Hold it close to your mouth, breathe warm upon it. Now look. Watch your own image, your own identity, waver in the steamy mirror. Or remember when someone mimicked your words, repeated them a few seconds later—tone and all. Now imagine someone mimicking your very essence. Feel crazy? So did Isaac—and Ishmael. The difficulty is that Ishmael is a cloudy mirror to Isaac, and vice versa. The problem is that neither son can grow up to be his own person unless they can grow up separately. The problem is not that the two brothers are so different; it is that they are so similar (though not identical). The danger is that their similarity will drive both of them crazy.

The similarity and the similar promises were God's profound joke—the joke at which both Isaac and Ishmael had to learn to laugh. From such a joke you can die laughing—or transform yourself and the world.

And today the joke remains unresolved. That is what we see before us now. Israelis and Palestinians love the same land. They cannot, either of them, bear to recognize that the other also loves the land. That the other also has a claim to the land. That the other is more like them than different. Each of them seems to feel that "if the other does, I don't." Neither seems able to grasp the possibility that the land has—somehow, somewhy—been promised twice.

And not only in relation to the land, but also in their experience of exile, there are some similarities. The Palestinians in their short exile have suffered a (milder) version of the torments that the Jews have suffered in their age-long exile. The Palestinians have even become the alternately upwardly mobile and downwardly victimized "Jews of the Middle East" (as many Arabs call them, with mixed respect, envy, and hatred—just as some Western Christians speak of the Jews).

Reconciliation? Living face to face? Let us come back to that after I explain how modern Zionism fits into the picture I have sketched.

In the last century there have been many modern Zionisms. Some have been explicitly religious, others explicitly secularist and antireligious. Some have been left wing, others right wing in their version of the new Jewish community they were building. (That should concern only Jews.) Some were fraternal, others domineering in their outlook on the Palestinian Arabs. (That must be of concern to everyone.)

All of them, even the ones that called themselves secular, drew on the religious-Jewish passion for the land of Israel; on the two millennia of Jewish prayers, three times a day, to return and there be permitted to build a holy society; on the knowledge that God's covenant with Israel had never been revoked and never would be—that the diaspora was both an exile and an education, was both in order that the Jews could learn God's teaching deeper and teach God's teaching better; and on the knowledge that someday the exile would end.

Is it possible for modern Christians or Muslims—for anyone except perhaps Palestinians who have been through a shorter version of the same exile—to understand this passion? Maybe. Try this. Imagine—if you empathized with the Vietnamese during the American war against them—that the United States had "won." Had poisoned the land and decimated the people and driven out those who were left. The Vietnamese, as those Americans who met them recognized with awe, loved their land with an awesome passion. How long would they have insisted on remembering it? How long would they have prayed, mourned, celebrated, walked, flown, in efforts to return? How long before they would have stopped planning to return? How long before others would have said they had no right to return? Twenty years? One hundred? Five hundred? Two thousand?

The Roman empire did that to the Jews. And the Jews remembered for two full thousand years. And not only remembered but planned, acted.

It is true that others—Christians and Muslims especially, out of religious theories of having supplanted the Jews—soon concluded that the Jews had lost any right to return. But that notion the Jews did not accept. Always, there were efforts to return.

To what end? So that the Jews should not remain forever *luftmenschen*, "air people," floating above reality, full of hot air, "spiritual" without mattering to material life. For the Jewish vision has always been that the most soulful holiness does not matter unless it is applied to "matter"—to body. The command to share out all the wealth and let the land rest in the year of Jubilee should not remain forever a lot of hot air blown across the lips of Torah scholars. Someday it must be done, and we need a land to do it with. Or fail to.

And here we come to the heart of the covenant, and why God promised the land twice. God wanted, wants, the Jews to be a holy people, a kingdom all of priests—a "vanguard" people, you might say. A holy people that teaches by example all the peoples how to be holy peoples.

Such a people needs a land to be holy with. That was why Martin Buber was a Zionist. He did not, in the beginning, want there to be a Jewish state, but he did want a self-governing Jewish community in the land of Israel. And when its history took the form of statehood, he acquiesced.

That need for a land is "right," as well as a responsibility, an obligation. And by giving the land of Israel to the people of Israel, God teaches that every people has a right, and an obligation, to a land on which it can live out its particular pattern of holiness. The Jewish people in its quest for self-determination in a land of its own is a vanguard for all the peoples—all of whom must, and may, seek self-determination in lands of their own. Palestinians too.

But surely each people to its own land? Palestinians to some land other than the land of Israel?

But the vanguard people has a special fate. A land for every people, a people for every land—yes. But the earth has no rigid "natural" boundaries between the lands and peoples. Every people must learn to share the earth with other peoples.

So the vanguard people must learn to share its land with another people. It may even be true—mysteriously true, mystically true, and geopolitically true as well—that only if the Jewish people learn to share its land with another people will the peoples of the earth learn to share the earth with each other in peace. And in our generation, it may even be true that if the Palestinians and Israelis cannot learn to live face to face with each other, the peoples of the earth may not live to work the earth at all. Perhaps it is no accident that many scenarios for World War Last begin with an Israeli-Palestinian collision.

And perhaps it is also no accident that the generation of human history in which the whole human race faces the truth that failing to share the great unboundaried earth may bring annihilation is the same generation in which the Jewish people returns to the land—and by its very arrival helps call into stronger distinctive reality its sister/brother people, the Palestinians. It is these contemporary synchronicities, fused with the ancient teachings of the Torah, that hint at God's presence in the story. For it is when God acts both in history and in the sparks of Holy Teaching that the Unity of the Universe seems most apparent.

Am I saying that God's promises to the children of Isaac and the children of Ishmael are the same? I doubt it. If we use both history and the human heart as guides to God's will, along with Torah, it seems to be that the kind of relationship the Jews and the Palestinians have to "that land" may not be the same. Jerusalem is unique to the Jews, very special but not absolutely unique to Muslims. The point that many Israelis make is also true: Arabs have many sovereign states, the Jews but one—can't Palestinian Arabs find some self-expression in the others? Some, it seems; but not enough. In other words, there may be differences between the promises. But that both peoples have a stake in the land seems obvious now—except to both of them.

Now suppose we come down to earth. What shall we do? (A Jewish question!)

For the Jewish people, the theology I have sketched above comes out this way: We must (1) build a holy society among ourselves in the land of Israel; (2) accept that Palestinians must have a place, should have a place within the land to build their own society under their own government (to me it seems clear that the West Bank and Gaza should be that place); and (3) celebrate the continuance of the diaspora in a dialectical and complementary relationship with the state of Israel.

And what should our cousins Ishmael do? They, the Palestinians, should begin by getting over their present unwillingness to acknowledge the right of the Jewish state to live in peace. I do not mean by accepting merely that Israel is, unfortunately, there to stay, but accepting that it should be there; that the existence of Israel, far from negating the Palestinians' right to self-determination in the same land, confirms that right. That Zionism is not necessarily racism, any more than the vision of Palestinian nationhood. Either can be turned into racism—or into sisterhood. And then the Palestinians should try to build their own society, by their own lights of holiness. Not for me to judge so long as they let Israel live in peace.

In the midst of the *intifada*, late in 1988, the Palestinians, through the Palestine National Council, seem, at long last, to have taken some major steps along the path that I have just described. (Not that they have gone as far on that path as would be possible, or helpful.) The Israeli government (as of June 1989) has taken only the tiniest step by proposing West Bank elections—and then all but negated that step by limiting the freedom, scope, and results of such elections. And meanwhile, by its attempt at physical repression of the *intifada*, the Israeli government has communicated not a readiness for transformation and reconciliation but an addiction to repression that has its own echoes in the Torah.

Those echoes are with the career of Mother Egypt as it tried both to give birth to the People Israel—and to prevent that birth. From *Mitzrayim* (Egypt), the "Narrow Place," came ultimately the birth that broke the waters of the Red Sea. But the birthpangs were made much worse—for Mother Egypt and First-born Israel—by Pharaoh's attempts to hold back the birth. Those attempts brought plague after plague down upon Egypt itself—and ultimately the death of Egypt's own first-born.

Why did Pharaoh act this way? At the beginning, out of fear of what the birth might mean to his and Egypt's power. As trouble mounted, he hardened his heart against the sufferings of both Egyptians and Israelites. He kept on choosing harshness.

And then he became addicted to the iron fist of repression. Says the Torah, he no longer chose, no longer hardened his own heart; *God* began to harden his heart. Reality, Truth, Inevitability took over. Once, twice, three times you may choose to smoke crack; but then you no longer choose, you are addicted. Even when Pharaoh's own advisers warned him that he was destroying his own Egypt, he could not stop himself.

As of June 1989, the Israeli government is somewhere on that self-destructive path. Many of its own citizens and of the Jewish people around the world are crying out in double pain—pain for the suffering of the Palestinians and pain for the plagues already descending upon Israel herself. Can the Israeli government still choose to take another path? Can the Jewish opposition make itself more effective than Pharaoh's advisers were?

It is easy to see why it is so hard for the Israeli government to change direction. The Torah's teachings point the way to understanding. Thirty-six times the Torah teaches the People Israel to love, respect, treat equally those who are "strangers" in the Land. Why? Because we know the heart of the stranger, because we were strangers in the narrow-minded land, *Mitzrayim*, Egypt. If this command came only once or twice its weight would be self-evident. But *36* times? This can only be because it was a hard teaching to learn. Those who had just suffered the terrible pains of slavery and genocide were in no mood for love or justice toward the stranger—any stranger. "We will enslave all strangers lest they gather the power to enslave us as the Egyptians did!" the people must have said, over and over.

So over and over, the Torah replied: "You must love the stranger as

yourself, not *despite*, but *because* you were strangers in the land of slavery."
This was not only the gentler, loving way; it was the path of self-protection,
for enslaving others leads to self-destruction. So it is easy to see why the
teaching was so hard to learn—and for some, it is also easy to see why the
teaching is so crucial to learn.

And so it is for Jews today, in the wake of the Nazi Holocaust and of
the bitter hostility of most of the Arab states and communities near Israel.
Easy to understand why the first response is the iron fist; easy to see how
hard it is to change; and for some, easy to see that the Torah's teaching
must be heard and change *must* come. Only by recognizing the aspect of
our selves that is attracted toward becoming Pharaoh can we in fact choose
not to become Pharaoh, not to act like Pharaoh.

These teachings are for Jews, and also for Palestinians. They too must
try to check their response to oppression—and turn it not toward repressing
others but toward reconciliation.

But those remarks are for us Jews and our cousins Ishmael. In this
volume I am not talking only to us or even to our cousins Ishmael.

What do I want of non-Palestinian Christians?

First, that they judge both Israel and the Palestinians by the same standards that they do all other peoples. It is for me to apply the high standards
of Torah to the behavior of the Jewish people. If, within our own territory,
we do not carry out the Jubilee, that is for us to struggle over. God may
throw us out of the land for our failures, but the Christian world should
be dealing with the beam in its own eye.

In our behavior to our neighbors, of course, everybody has a stake, Christians too. But even there, the standards that Christians apply to the Jews
should not be higher than those they apply to anyone else. For example:
In 1982 the Israeli assault on Palestinians in Lebanon seemed very bad—
but so was what King Hussein did to the Palestinians in Jordan in 1971. In
1989, Israeli repression of the *intifada* is disgusting; but so has been the
Syrian repression of Palestinians living in Lebanon. I, a Jew, am in spiritual
agony and political rebellion over the failure of the Jewish state to live up
to Jewish standards—and I have both the right and duty to be so. But why
do some Christians seem more pained and far more vocal about it when it
is Israel repressing the Palestinians than when it was Jordan or Syria?

Among Jews there is a deep suspicion that many Christians disguise their
dislike, even their hatred, of the Jewish people behind an insistence that
we Jews are noble. So noble as to be utterly dastardly when we fail to be
noble.

I do not ask Christians to condone or ignore any oppressive acts that
Israel may take against other peoples. I do not ask for extra moral credit
for Jews because of the Holocaust, or anything else. But I do ask Christians
to ask themselves whether they are putting Jews on a moralistic pedestal
as a first step toward dragging us in the mud afterward.

Secondly, I would ask Christians to affirm vigorously that the Jewish people does have a right to govern itself in the land of Israel. That right does not include the right to oppress another people, but even if we oppress another people we do not lose the right to govern ourselves. The American people, for all the horrible destruction their government visited upon the Vietnamese—far worse than what Israel has so far done to the Palestinians—did not thereby forfeit their right to govern themselves.

Of course I understand the psychology by which others, whenever we behave oppressively, may get angry enough to suggest that such behavior cancels our right to be ourselves at all. But just because I understand the psychology does not mean I condone it. Only if we feel secure, affirmed by others in our right to be ourselves, will we feel secure enough to be self-critical and to hear others' criticisms.

That is why it would make a great difference to the readiness of many Jews to listen to criticism if they discover that there are Christians who are prepared to affirm with great intensity the Jewish right of self-government in the land of Israel, and simultaneously to insist that we not abuse that right by oppressing others. To many Jews, the Christian churches seem to be divided into two camps.

On one hand, heavily secularized liberals who criticize Israel unjustly, side always with the Palestinians, have their doubts about the fundamental covenant beneath the Jewish state and, if you scratch them hard enough, confess that on universalist grounds they don't like the idea of a Jewish state anyway, and would rather have one that is "secular democratic"; and perhaps—this is our fantasy, at least—if you scratch still harder will finally mutter that God's covenant with the Jews was annulled 2,000 years ago anyway. And on the other hand, fundamentalists or evangelicals who celebrate the Jewish state and don't care a damn for the Palestinians.

It would be a new thing for serious Christians to affirm the continuing covenant of the people Israel with God, to celebrate the Jewish people's recovery of its ability to govern itself in the land of Israel, and at the same time to affirm that the Palestinians, children in the body and the spirit of Abraham through Ishmael and Mohammed, also have God's promise of some sort, out of which grows the right to govern themselves in part of the same land.

It would be a new thing, an unsettling thing—to some Jews an annoyance, to some an affliction, to some an attraction, to all an incitement to new thinking.

I do believe that if someone else can steadfastly see both the children of Ishmael and the children of Isaac, that will help us see each other face to face, not as in a dark and cloudy mirror. I do not promise that it will be soon, or easy. The story was first lived, and written, about 4,000 years ago. But perhaps the endtime of this story is at last upon us, as world disaster or as reconciliation.

PART III

A CRITICAL DIALOGUE: JEWISH AND CHRISTIAN PERSPECTIVES

7

False Messianism and Prophetic Consciousness

Toward a Liberation Theology of Jewish-Christian Solidarity

ROSEMARY RADFORD RUETHER

Christianity traditionally regarded Judaism as a religion of obsolete particularism, tied to the idea of God's election of a particular people and land. This particularism, it believed, had been superceded by the fuller revelation of God in Christ, through whom redemption is extended to all peoples of the earth. Thus one of the major conflicts between Christianity and Judaism, traditionally, is the different way each constructs the relationship of the universality of God—and God's message—to the particularity of an elect people who are the receivers of and historical witnesses to that message.

JUDAISM: ETHNOCENTRIC AND UNIVERSAL TENDENCIES

In Hebrew scripture and rabbinic teaching, Judaism can be perceived as having two tendencies in relation to the other peoples or nations: an ethnocentric tendency, which calls Israel to separate itself from the other nations, and a universal trend, which extends salvation to the nations. The covenant of God with Israel binds Israel to the worship of the one God and separates it from the idolatry of the nations. The laws given by God to Israel separate Israel from the abominations of the nations. Israel is to become a sphere of holiness, over against the unholiness and pollution of the nations, precisely by observing these walls of separation. The final salvation of Israel can be viewed as a triumph over the nations. Israel will rule over the nations and reduce them to servitude to its hegemonic rule over the earth (the Middle East). At its most judgmental, the nations are marked down for destruction on the day of judgment (Zech. 12:9, 14:16-19).

The universalist trend, on the other hand, sees all the nations coming to redemption through Israel. For Isaiah that suggests that all nations will become proselytes to the God of Israel and, in some sense, the law of Israel. From this submission will flow universal peace:

> It shall come to pass in the latter days that the mountain of the Lord shall be established as the highest of all the mountains . . . and all nations shall flow to it and many people shall come and say, "Come let us go up to the Mountain of the Lord, to the house of the God of Jacob, that he may teach us his ways and that we may walk in his paths, for out of Zion shall go forth the law and the word of the Lord from Jerusalem." [Isa. 2:2-3]

In the book of Jonah the ethnocentric trend is criticized by telling the story of a nationalist prophet who desires God to punish and destroy Israel's enemies. But God, in turn, forces Jonah to be the instrument of God's mercy and forgiveness upon those enemies, the Ninevites. The clear message of the story is that God has created and desires to save all nations. What is less clear is exactly what is meant by the Ninevites having repented of their evil ways. This seems to be thought of in a more general way as conversion from ethical evil, from the "violence that is in their hand," rather than a specific conversion to Judaism. A monotheistic concept of God, shared by both nations—Israel and Assyria—seemed implied.

Despite these longings for salvation, often expressed as political hegemony over the other nations, ancient Israel was, for almost all its history, subject to the other great empires around it: Egypt, Assyria, Babylonia, Persia, the Hellenistic and then the Roman empires. Indeed its conception of salvation as deliverance from the power of these empires expressed this context. With the advent of the Hellenistic empires in the late fourth century, Israel encountered a colonialist who desired not only political hegemony, but also the cultural assimilation of its subjects. For the Greeks, the Hellene, the free Greek male, was the norm of true humanity, in contrast to servile people, women and slaves, and non-Hellenes or barbarians. To be a Hellene was a matter of culture, not race. Becoming a Hellene was a *paideia*, assimilation into a culture that could be taught and learned.

Hellenistic cultural universalism was both attractive and deeply threatening to Jews of this period. The pietist element of the Maccabean revolt of the second century B.C.E. represented an effort to purge this growing Hellenistic influence from Jewish life. But the Hasmonean kings who came to power were often resistant students of their Hasidic mentors.[1] Their precarious survival for one hundred years depended on alliances with one advancing imperial power, Rome, against the resident Hellenistic empires. At the same time, Jewish intellectuals absorbed and adapted Greek literary and philosophical learning. In Alexandria, Philo, the flower of Hellenistic Judaism, created a synthesis of Torah and middle Platonism in the first century C.E. For Philo, the particularities of Jewish life, the Torah, the temple, the observances of daily life, were the outward sacramental expressions of an inward universal mystery expressed in the language of Platonic mysticism. The universal and the particular were reconciled by a relation of outward manifestation embodying inward cosmic truth.[2]

The rabbinic teachers, who salvaged and reconstituted Jewish life after the loss of the temple and the city of Jerusalem in 70 and 136 C.E., also adapted elements of Hellenistic thought. Jews were called all the more to separate themselves from the nations by becoming a holy people, observant of the laws of God. But the movement from being born a Jew to becoming an observant Jew was formulated as a *paideia*, a culture that was learned through study. Jewish peoplehood thus became a portable *paideia*, one that could be carried and planted anywhere among the nations, no longer dependent on possession of a homeland, the temple cult and priesthood, or political sovereignty.[3] These things were fixed in memory and in hope through study. The path to their future messianic restoration lay through the school that would shape the Jewish people to become fully obedient to God's commandments. As in Isaiah, that eventual restoration was also understood to include the redemption of the nations.

EARLY CHRISTIANITY AND THE REFORMATION

Christianity, on the other hand, shaped itself over against its Pharisaic rival in the first to fourth centuries C.E. by a synthesis of the Jewish messianic and Hellenistic traditions. Christianity began as a messianic sect that saw itself as the people of a crucified and resurrected messiah who awaited his imminent return to judge the nations and gather the redeemed into the new age to come. It soon expanded into a proselytizing mission throughout the Greco-Roman Empire and, even beyond its borders, into the Persian world. It quickly absorbed Hellenistic allegorical exegesis in which historical realities are the external signs of inward spiritual meaning. Both of these kinds of spiritual and apocalyptic universalism were brought together to situate itself over against rabbinic Judaism. In New Testament books, such as Hebrews, and also in the writings of the church fathers, Judaism was defined as the anticipatory and carnal outward letter over against that which has been fulfilled on the spiritual and universal level in Christianity.[4]

As Christianity moved from being a persecuted sect to the established imperial religion, its relation to Judaism became triumphalistic and punitive. Christianity came to see itself as the new universal people of God drawn from all nations. The ingathering of all nations to Zion had already taken place in the church. The Jews alone were the pariah people. They had rejected and killed their messiah. Like Cain they were to be a protected but also a cursed and marked people within Christian society. They were to remain exiles and wanderers under servitude to God's new people, the Christians, until the end of history. They were never to return to their land or rebuild their temple. Their law was obsolete and without salvific power. Yet their election remained, in a negative sense. God was preserving them for that future end of days when Elijah would return and they would accept Jesus as their messiah.[5] Thus Christianity reversed the relation of Israel and the nations. The nations were already being gathered into Zion. Only Israel remained outside, to be gathered in as part of the eschatological culmination of history. Reconciliation of Israel and the church was assured, on Christian terms.

The Reformation, particularly the Calvinist tradition, saw a significant reinterpretation of this relationship of the church and Israel. The Reformation saw the fragmentation of the remnants of Christian universalist empire into competing Christian nation-states, divided by competing Christian allegiances. Allegorical interpretation was replaced by literal historical interpretation of scripture. It was no longer possible to think of the people of Israel, the land of Israel, as preliminary signs of universal spiritual truths. They became real contemporary entities; a particular people, a particular land with real historical location.

Competing nation-states with their nationalized state-churches each began to define themselves as the new Israel, in an ethnocentric sense. The English, the French, the Spanish each saw themselves as God's elect nation, chosen to rebuke the infidels, in the form of separated Christians, and to convert the heathen, in the form of new peoples of Asia, Africa, and the Americas coming under the sway of their colonial expansion. For the Puritan tradition particularly this created a significantly changed view of the relation of the Christian national new Israel to the old Israel. The Catholic saints were dismissed as religious ancestors, and instead the biblical Hebrews became one's religious forebears. Contemporary Jews were seen as the representatives of those ancient Hebrews. They represented God's continuing election of the old Israel, as the foundation of God's new elect people—that is, the English or the American new Israel.

In the seventeenth century this new sense of relationship of the new and old Israel was expressed in a widespread belief that the new Israel should sponsor the restoration of the old Israel to its national homeland. There the Jews would regain national sovereignty over their land and rebuild the temple. Thus Protestantism reclaimed the particularistic elements of Jewish future promise, which had been discarded by traditional Catholic spiritualized universalism. Protestants believed that these particularistic promises of God to the Jews must be fulfilled first and then would come universal judgment and redemption of the world through Christ.[6]

For Protestants this redemption for the Jews was still premised on conversion to Christ. Protestants believed that the Reformation had cleansed

Christianity of its false accretions. It was these false accretions that had prevented the conversion of the Jews. Once purified of Catholic error, the Jews would see the light and be converted to Christianity. Then the Christians would restore them to their ancient homeland. But when the Jews failed to be converted to Protestant Christianity, this eschatological timetable was revised. Instead it began to be said that the restoration of the Jews, in their unbelieving state, must take place first. Once they were restored to their land, and had rebuilt the temple, there would be a period of tribulation in which the Antichrist and the false prophet would mislead the Jews and the world.

At the critical moment, Christ would return as conquering messiah, the one hundred forty-four thousand Jews, twelve thousand from each of the twelve tribes of Israel, would be gathered into the Christian fold, along with the elect of the nations (Rev. 7:4-9). These elect would be raptured to the heavens, while the Antichrist is defeated and the earth purged of evil. Then the elect would return to reign with Christ for a thousand years. This is the form in which Jewish restorationism was understood among English and American evangelicals in the late nineteenth century and is still substantially the same eschatology held by pro-Zionist Christian fundamentalists today.[7]

These ideas of restoration were strongly resisted by Jews in the nineteenth century who saw these efforts as religious garb for a program of deportation of Jews from western Europe and America at a time (1880-1910) when they were pouring into this area to escape from Russian pogroms.[8] It would not be until the late 1970s that the Zionist establishment would begin to see the usefulness of an alliance with these millennialist Christians in their project of defending what was now an established Jewish state.[9]

In the late nineteenth century there emerged in various forms a Jewish movement of return to Palestine, with the aim of building a Jewish majority in the land and finally establishing Jewish political sovereignty. The Zionist movement was responding to two threats to Jewish identity, as that identity had been shaped by rabbinic teaching in the Diaspora for eighteen hundred years. One was the dissolution of the walls of the ghetto by the Enlightenment and Jewish emancipation. Reform Judaism adapted to this new situation by dropping most of the laws of daily life that had set the Jewish community apart, and reconstituting Judaism as a private religious choice that could coexist with other privatized religious options in the context of the secular state. For many Jews this reform was only an intermediate step to complete assimilation.

On the other hand, Jewish emancipation met a new European nationalism, which declared that Jews were a nation, a race, not a religion, and as such were fundamentally unassimilable into a racially identified French, or German, or other European nationalism. Zionism was shaped between the hammer and the anvil of these two clashing European relations to the

Jews. It remained a minority movement among Western Jews until the Second World War. Orthodox Judaism rejected it as an attempt to do by unholy means what could be done only by the messiah. For them it was forbidden to "force the end" or rebel against the sovereignty of the nations over Palestine in nonmessianic times and by secular means.[10] Reform Judaism also rejected Zionism. For them it was an apostasy to the faith of the Enlightenment that Jews and other people could live side by side within many nations through a separation of religion from secular nationality.

JUDAISM AND ZIONISM

In spite of the secular and even atheistic views of most Zionist leaders, and the rejection of Zionism by most of religious Judaism, there has gradually emerged a synthesis of Judaism and Zionism, particularly in the last twenty years, since the 1967 war. This increasing prominence of religious Zionism is necessitated by the fact that Zionism, despite its secularity, is ultimately based on two religious propositions: (1) that God promised this region to the Jews as a permanent possession, even if they are not present in it, and (2) that return to the land is a redemptive event. These religious premises are vital both to cementing the loyalty of world Jewry to the state of Israel and also drawing support from a substantial portion of Protestantized European and American Christianity (including much of post-Vatican II Catholicism), which shares these same premises.

One can briefly encapsulate the development of Jewish religious Zionism in two figures: Rabbi Abraham Kook, Ashkenazi chief rabbi of Palestine under the British mandate, and his son, Rabbi Zvi Yehudah Kook, one of the mentors of the *Gush Emunim*. Abraham Kook drew on the traditions of kabbalistic messianism. The cosmos was seen as rent and fragmented by a cosmic fall into evil. The sparks of light that represent broken divine unity are fragmented in the realm of chaos and darkness. Kook understood these sparks of light as the souls of Jews scattered in the gentile nations. The land of Israel was understood to have, by its very nature, a kind of superior status of holiness than other parts of the earth. It was the center of the cosmos, closer to God, one might almost say in an umbilical relation to the divine matrix.

For Abraham Kook the very ingathering of Jews to the land, even under secular auspices, was a redemptive event. It represented the ingathering of light to its divine center. The secular ingathering of the Jews must lead on to shaping an observant Jewish community in Palestine. Torah would become the law of the Jewish state. Israel must become a holy nation, a nation that would transcend the force and violence that characterized other nations in their relations to one another. Through the healing of Israel would also come the healing of the nations. The other nations would beat their swords into pruning hooks and come to live in peace with one another through the example of Israel.[11]

This cosmic vision of the healing of the nation, through the ingathering of Israel to its homeland and its renewal as a holy nation, has been translated into much more militant and ethnocentric terms by Kook's son, Rabbi Zvi Yehudah Kook and the *Gush Emunim*.[12] This group has been at the forefront of the armed settler movement. They have forced the creation of new settlements in the occupied territories. They have also been behind militant Yeshiva students who seek to expand the Jewish section of the Old City of Jerusalem around the temple mount, aiming ultimately at a takeover of the temple mount itself from its present Muslim guardians. These settlements have been very much supported by Christian fundamentalists, whose eschatology includes the necessity of resettling the whole of ancient *Eretz Israel*, as defined by the book of Joshua, and the rebuilding of the temple.[13]

In 1947 the United Nations divided the British mandate for Palestine into a Jewish and an Arab state. The portion that it allocated to the Jews had almost as many Palestinian Arabs as Jews resident in it. The Palestinians and Arabs rejected this partition in favor of a Palestinian Arab state in the whole area, within which Jews could be citizens. Zionist leadership had long recognized that, in order to create a Jewish state—that is, a state where Jews would be the overwhelming majority and only full citizens—it was necessary not only to sponsor major immigration of Jews, but also to expel the majority of the Palestinian population. During the 1948 war, the boundaries of the Jewish state were expanded to about twenty percent more territory than that granted by the United Nations, and some 780,000 out of the 900,000 Palestinians that had lived in this region were made refugees. Needless to say this expulsion was planned by the Israelis, specifically Ben-Gurion. It was *not* called for by the Arab states.[14] The state of Israel has refused ever since to repatriate these refugees.

In 1967 Israel conquered the rest of the mandate area, and thus has ruled as an occupying army over another group of Palestinians who now number 1.5 million. Together with the Palestinians in Israel, who have grown by natural increase to about 715,000, Israel now rules over more than two million Palestinians, with a Jewish population of about three million. Since this threatens the demography of a Jewish state, Israel has wished to rule this region without annexing it and granting these Palestinians citizenship. The result has been a spiral of repression and resistance that, in December of 1987, broke out in massive sustained protest. The violence of repression has likewise escalated. Between December 7, 1977, and April 18, 1988, over 225 Palestinians were killed and over 30,000 severely injured by live ammunition, rubber bullets, clubs, and cyanide tear gas.[15] In the process, the consensus theology that had allowed Jews to avert their eyes from the true history of Israel and regard it in the mythological clothings of a redemptive return and the beginning of a messianic future has become unraveled.

I suggest that the messianic Zionist theology that has dominated Jewish life for the last twenty years is proving to be a false messianism. Christians and Jews, who have bought into that theology as the basis of Jewish-Christian dialogue, are becoming increasingly defensive and hostile to criticism. The Jewish community that has bought the Zionist consensus, and its cadre of Christian supporters, are very angry people, not wishing to face up to the way they have been misled, preferring to project their anger outward at what they see as a wall of hatred of the outside world. The failures of the state of Israel to be a messianic, utopian state is to be blamed on this externalized hatred. The labels "self-hating Jew" or "anti-Semite" are the responses to efforts of Jews or others to break out of this defensive wall with a more truthful historical account of Israel's history in the Middle East.

I believe that there can be no authentic Jewish-Christian dialogue on the basis of this Zionist consensus theology. A dialogue based on this theology has painted itself into a corner of pandering and mutual manipulation. Jewish-Christian dialogue, if it is to be authentic, must be refounded on a new basis. This basis I call a liberation theology of Jewish-Christian solidarity.[16]

The Jewish community has moved in forty years from a period of greatest victimization to very considerable power, both as a state with the fourth largest army in the world, including nuclear weapons, in Israel, and very considerable global power, particularly in the United States. But it has tended to promote and secure this power, and cover up the inevitable mistakes of power, by constant evocation of the experience of ultimate victimization, the Holocaust. This evocation of the specter of ultimate annihilation serves both to terrorize Jews and strike guilt into Christians, and silence both from any thoughts of seeing, much less speaking, the problematics about the state of Israel. A collaboration of the Jewish and Christian establishments has been developed, a kind of right-wing ecumenism, in which each helps to repress the critics and dissenters in the other community. The Jewish establishment aids the Vatican in its repression of Third World liberation theologians, and the Christian establishment refrains from publishing or listening to Jewish dissenters from the Zionist consensus, such as Israeli human rights activist, Israel Shahak.[17]

The new dialogue must start with a recognition that, however much Jews have kept alive a religious longing for return to their biblical homeland, the state of Israel, as it has actually been built, has been tied first to British and then to American imperialism. The relation it has established with the Palestinian Arabs is substantially that of a colonialist occupying power, which has taken the land of the indigenous people, either expelling them or subjugating them as a pool of landless proletarian labor.[18]

Once that truth is recognized, then one can ask how Israel can be salvaged, not to become a messianic state, but simply to become a more credible expression of ordinary justice, more on the model of a noncolonial social democracy, like Sweden, less on the model of an apartheid military state, like South Africa. I will not attempt to go into details about how that might happen; that would be the matter of a different paper. Basically what this would mean is accepting either a bi-national or two-state solution with the Palestinians, and gradually liberating itself from dependency on American foreign aid, and thus American global imperialism.

A NEW THEOLOGY OF JEWISH-CHRISTIAN SOLIDARITY

I wish to conclude this essay with some reflections on what a new theology of Jewish-Christian solidarity might mean. First of all, it means that Jews and Christians approach each other as peer communities, both of which have gained power, both of whom have abused power to oppress others, even though that history is much more recent for Jews than for Christians. Although Christians need to be well aware of their history of victimization of Jews and seek to remedy Christian practices that continue such victimization, for the most part, Jews and Christians today do not meet as victim and victimizer, but as two historical people with some power and some of the failures of power. They need to understand this new relationship, not as competitive put-downs, but as a mutual quest to strengthen the ethical prophetic traditions of each community, against tendencies to self-sacralization or false messianism.

This means, on the one hand, a Jewish recovery of its prophetic voice vis-à-vis the world Zionist establishment and government of Israel. It means that Christian prophetic theology, which has been rediscovered in Third World liberation theologies, must see itself in solidarity with the Jews, both in critique of anti-Jewish elements of the Christian tradition, and also as a people who, like the church, need to be called into solidarity with the poor and the despised. This solidarity with the poor and despised includes marginalized people within the Jewish community; Jewish women, oriental Jews in Israel, and also oppressed people outside the Jewish community, which Jewish power discomfits, particularly Palestinians. Christians stand not in self-righteous judgment, but in solidarity with this quest to reclaim a Jewish prophetic voice. For any sins of Jews in such matters, Christians have been guilty of a thousandfold.

This liberation theology of Jewish-Christian solidarity might meet on the ground of a mutual critique of false messianism. Judaism traditionally regarded the Christian claim that Jesus was the Christ as a false messianism, a splitting of spiritual redemption from historico-ethical reality. One pretends that redemption has already arrived when, in fact, the historical realities of continuing evil indicate that the world is unredeemed. I will leave aside the additional Jewish critique of divine-man christology as idolatry and concentrate only on this question of fulfilled or unfulfilled messianic hope.

It seems to me that the Jewish no to Christian messianism has been correct. Jewish messianism has always meant a real ethical transformation of the conduct of society in history. As long as war and injustice remain, the world is unredeemed. Christianity, particularly in the last eighty years, through a recovered understanding of what the Jewish tradition actually meant by the word messiah, has come to acknowledge this unredeemed nature of the world. They have remodeled christology in proleptic terms. They have come to see Jesus not as fulfiller of Jewish messianic hopes, but as a messianic prophet, one who denounces oppression and injustice, and announces the reign of God. Crucified by the systems of religious and political injustice, he is resurrected in hope, to remain in Christian memory as a pointer to God's future of justice and peace, who renews our struggle against evil in the world. This is a christology that makes sense to the Jewish tradition of ethical realism. Although they would see no particular reason why they need to relate to Jesus as bearer of this message, since they have substantially this same message from the prophets.

The Zionist consensus theology of the last twenty years represents a more recent, I suspect short-lived, entrapment of the Jewish community in a political version of false messianism. Zionism claimed to be building a world of justice and peace by means that could only lead to increasing injustice and war. The questioning of the Zionist redemptive myths of return from *Galut* (exile) and the beginning of the messianic age must create a shift in the relationship of Israel as a world community to the state of Israel. The two will have to be distinguished, rather than identified, as Zionist ideology has sought to do. To be an Israeli is the nationality of a minority of Jews (20 percent), plus some three-quarters of a million Palestinian Muslims and Christians. The people of Israel remain a world community who belong to many nations, one of which is the state of Israel. As a political project of one part of the Jewish people, the state of Israel remains a special concern of the Jewish people, but it is not their global nationality or destiny.[19]

This normalizing of the state of Israel as a nation-state, and one that must become increasingly pluralistic, recognizing the full citizenship of Palestinian Arabs within it, as well as a Palestinian nation alongside it, means that one applies the ordinary ethical yardsticks of unredeemed time to it. One recognizes that, like all nations, it is unholy and unrighteous. One calls it to become a more just state, as one calls all nations today to become more just; less riddled by racist, classist, sexist, and colonialist systems of injustice.

The critique of false messianism basically calls for a shift in the way the ideal is related to the real. In false messianism the ideal is used to cover up the faults of the real, to clothe the real in the garments of redemptive perfection. Truthful description of reality is rejected in the name of the ideal, and those who seek to speak the truth are persecuted as heretics. Liberation from false messianism, for both Jews and Christians, means a renewal of prophetic consciousness. Prophetic consciousness represents a shift in the perception of the relation of the ideal and the real. Instead of the ideal serving to cover over and falsify the real, the ideal becomes a critical yardstick to judge the true achievements and failures of the real. It also motivates continued work of reform and amelioration of the real, by reference to these ideals.

Prophetic consciousness presupposes a certain trust and confidence in the truthfulness and goodness of ultimate reality and one's own relation to it. One cannot judge reality without a firm place to stand. Thus part of what can restore prophetic consciousness, vis-à-vis the failures of the state of Israel, is a renewed confidence in the ultimate grounding of Jewish peoplehood, which does not need the "good works" of the state of Israel to justify its "right to exist" or to protect it from annihilation. In reality, the relationship of Zionism toward the safety of Jews in the Diaspora has been ambivalent. Today it is hardly realistic to think of the state of Israel as a place where all Jews can go to be safe.[20] Any new annihilation that would seriously endanger the Jewish people would take the whole planet with it. We are all in this together. The Holocaust, as a specifically Jewish tragedy, cannot be repeated. The next holocaust can be the holocaust of us all. Jewish annihilation or survival cannot be separated from human annihilation or survival.

Thus Jews and Christians stand today not as particular to universal, and not simply as powerless to powerful, but as two historical communities, each with their histories of power and powerlessness, each with their hopes and their realities of failures. Christians, although many times larger and somewhat more culturally diverse, are nevertheless one limited historical community among others. The renewal of other great historical religions — Islam, Judaism, Buddhism — the renewal of non-Western cultures in the process of liberation from Western colonialism, means that the whole world will never become all Christian. Christianity must give up its world-conquering mission.

The many distinct cultural communities of humanity need to enter into solidarity with each other in a way that can affirm cultural distinctiveness, and yet hold each other morally accountable for our mutual survival on the one earth we all call home. The unity of the planet points toward a One God, the source of the world, the parent of all nations, not in the sense of demanding that all nations convert to one religion, but in the sense of making us siblings in one human family. Our source and goal in this one earth, and its God, calls us to end our sibling rivalry and realize our solidarity as a family of many peoples who must together become caretakers of one earth.[21]

NOTES

1. One group of Hasidim became the Essenes who regarded the Hasmonean priest-kings as the Wicked Priest who had led the nation into apostasy: see Geza Vermes, *The Dead Sea Scrolls in English* (Baltimore: Penguin, 1962), pp. 63-65.

Another group of Hasidim, the Pharisees, remained in the Hasmonean court and struggled to subjugate the kings to their sway: see Jacob Neusner, *From Politics to Piety: The Emergence of Pharisaic Judaism* (New York: Ktav, 1979), p. 64.

2. E. R. Goodenough, *By Light, Light: The Mystic Gospel of Hellenistic Judaism* (New Haven: Yale University Press, 1935).

3. Ellis Rivkin, *The Shaping of Jewish History* (New York: Scribner, 1971), pp. 42-83.

4. Rosemary Ruether, *Faith and Fratricide: The Theological Roots of Anti-Semitism* (New York: Seabury, 1979), pp. 107-11, 149-60.

5. Ibid., 144-49, 185-86.

6. Regina S. Sharif, *Non-Jewish Zionism: Its Roots in Western History* (London: Zed, 1983), pp. 9-32.

7. David A. Rausch, *Zionism Within Early American Fundamentalism, 1878-1919* (New York: Edwin Mellen Press, 1979); also Ronald R. Stockton, "Christian Zionism—Prophecy and Public Opinion," *Middle East Journal*, vol. 41, no. 2 (Spring 1987): 234-54.

8. Rausch, *Zionism*, pp. 88-95.

9. Merrill Simon, *Jerry Falwell and the Jews* (New York: Jonathan David Publishers, 1984).

10. See Klaus Herrmann, "Politics and Divine Promise," in *Judaism or Zionism: What Difference for the Middle East?* (London: Zed, 1986), pp. 29-30.

11. Arthur Hertzberg, *The Zionist Idea: A Historical Analysis and Reader* (New York: Meridian, 1960), pp. 416-31; also Abraham Isaac Kook, *The Lights of Penitence*, translation and introduction by Ben Zion Kokser (New York: Paulist Press, 1978).

12. See Uriel Tal, "The Land and the State of Israel in Israeli Religious Life," *Proceedings of the Rabbinical Assembly of the 76th Annual Convention*, 38:1-40 (New York: Rabbinical Association, 1977).

13. Grace Halsell, *Prophecy and Politics: Militant Evangelists on the Road to Nuclear War* (Westport, Conn.: Lawrence Hill, 1986).

14. See Michael Palumbo, *The Palestinian Catastrophe: The 1948 Expulsion of a People from Their Homeland* (London: Faber and Faber, 1987).

15. These figures come from the Database Project on Palestinian Human Rights, P.O. Box 20479, Jerusalem.

16. I owe this analysis particularly to Marc Ellis in private communications and public conversations. See his *Toward a Jewish Theology of Liberation* (Maryknoll, N.Y.: Orbis Books, 1987), pp. 111-12.

17. The analysis of the role of the Jewish establishment in repression of Catholic liberation theologians was presented at the Harvard Divinity School, March 8, 1988, by Marc Ellis in a forum on solidarity among liberation theologies. For the treatment of Israel Shahak, see Rosemary Ruether, "Zionism and the Ideological Manipulation of Christian Groups," *American-Arab Affairs* (Fall 1987), no. 22: 63-68.

18. See Ian Lustick, *Arabs in the Jewish State: Israel's Control of a National Minority* (Austin: University of Texas, 1980), for the status of Palestinian Arabs who are citizens of Israel. For the legal situation of Palestinians in the West Bank, see Raja Shehadeh, *Occupier's Law: Israel and the West Bank* (Washington, D.C.: Institute for Palestine Studies, 1985).

19. For an analysis of the contradictions of the Zionist claims to be the nationality

of all Jews, see Akiva Orr, *The UnJewish State: The Politics of Identity in Israel* (London: Ithaca Press, 1983). See also the recently released *Statement of Principles of Conservative Judaism* (Jewish Theological Seminary in America, 1988), pp. 34-39.

20. There are presently eighteen million Jews in the world, only three million of whom regularly reside in Israel (about 0.5 million Israeli citizens live permanently abroad with dual citizenship). The communal conflicts created by the occupation of the West Bank and Gaza Strip make it evident that Israel cannot actually accommodate the immigration of all of world Jewry. Moreover, Zionism has historically favored the building of the state of Israel over actual safety and welfare of Jews in the Diaspora. For a striking example of this, see Edwin Black, *The Transfer Agreement: The Untold Story of the Secret Agreement between the Third Reich and Jewish Palestine* (New York: Macmillan, 1984).

21. The historical analysis and ethical and theological reflections in this paper represent a summary of a book published by Harper and Row in 1989, *The Wrath of Jonah: Religion and Nationalism in the Israeli-Palestinian Conflict*, by Rosemary R. Ruether, with Herman J. Ruether.

8

Jews, Israel, and Liberation Theology

RICHARD L. RUBENSTEIN

No contemporary movement in Christian theology has aroused as much interest as liberation theology. Given the tendency of major theological movements within Christianity to influence Jewish thinkers, it was almost inevitable that some Jewish thinkers would explore the relevance of liberation theology for Jewish theology. A beginning has been made by Marc H. Ellis and Rabbi Dan Cohn-Sherbok.[1] Of the two efforts, Ellis's contribution has had the greater impact, in part because the positions he adopts are far more radical than those of Cohn-Sherbok.

Marc Ellis is a member of the faculty of the Maryknoll School of Theology. He is also a member of Rabbi Michael Robinson's reform congregation. Ellis describes himself as "a student of contemporary religious thought rather than a trained theologian." As is indicated by the title of his book, *Toward a Jewish Theology of Liberation*, he has not written a Jewish liberation theology, but has attempted to spell out the spiritual, intellectual, and political preconditions that "might give birth" to such a theology.

Although Ellis describes himself as a practicing Jew, most of his work and study has been with what he describes as "progressive Roman Catholic groups and institutions." He received his Ph.D. from Marquette University. He has written an extremely interesting book entitled *A Year at the Catholic Worker*, describing his experiences in that institution and now teaches at the intellectual and spiritual center of liberation theology in North America, the Maryknoll School of Theology. Although Ellis writes that his affiliations might evoke "fear or wonder," they aroused neither in me. I have known and admired Ellis since he was an undergraduate student in religion at my university.

Admiration and respect do not imply agreement. Ellis has presented a theological and political critique of both Israel and the American Jewish community that is far harsher and, I believe, far more unrealistic, than

96

anything suggested by the vast majority of those Jewish intellectuals and activists on the left who are involved in the Jewish community.

According to Ellis, the "dialectic of slavery and liberation" is at the heart of Jewish life. That dialectic is derived from the experience of the Exodus from Egypt. While acknowledging that there has been "fidelity to covenantal values" in contemporary Jewish life, Ellis complains that "the Jewish community's struggle to be faithful to those values has been shadowed by the reality of *betrayal*, for in advance of our own interests, we have been slave merchants and masters, supported corrupt kings and governments, and even at times oppressed one another" (italics added).

The theme of Jewish *betrayal* of Judaism's ideals runs through Ellis's exposition. Some may regard Ellis's accusation of *betrayal* as a contemporary expression of the prophets' denunciation of Israel's want of faithfulness to its divinely bestowed covenant. Others, myself included, see it as extraordinarily insensitive to Jewish feelings and a misreading of history, which tends toward a more charitable interpretation of the conduct of Israel's antagonists than of Israel itself. According to Webster, the primary meaning of betrayal is "to deliver to an enemy *by treachery or fraud,* in violation of trust," as would be the case when an officer betrays his native city. A second meaning is "to be a traitor; to prove faithless or treacherous to, as to a trust or one who trusts; to fail or desert in a moment of need."

Ellis's insensitive use of the term is indicative of why *Toward a Jewish Theology of Liberation* is not likely to be the beginning of a dialogue on a new Jewish theology. No matter what the shortcomings of the Jewish community, no theological writing will receive a serious hearing that repeats, albeit unintentionally, the kind of anti-Jewish defamations that in the past have led to the casting of Jews wholly outside any shared universe of moral obligation with their neighbors.[2] That Jews, like most other peoples, have often fallen short of their highest ideals, that some have from time to time been rebellious and disobedient, is beyond dispute. Such failings place them within the normal spectrum of human behavior. But the accusation of *betrayal* carries with it altogether different associations. The ascription of betrayal and treason as fundamental Jewish characteristics has its roots in the image of Judas Iscariot betraying his master for money with a kiss. Implied in that image is the not so subliminal message that, as Judas utilized a loving act to betray Jesus for money, so the Jews are not to be trusted even when they give the appearance of fidelity. This image has been imparted for millennia to young Christians with all the esthetic and emotional resources available to the church when the individual is least capable of rationally evaluating his or her information intake. The image of the Jew as betrayer has done almost as much as the Christkiller accusation to cast the Jew wholly outside any conceivable universe of moral obligation with Christians, especially in times of stress.[3]

Ellis would under no circumstances intentionally lend support to anti-Semitic defamation of the Jewish people. Unfortunately, this does not exclude the possibility of unintentional insensitivity. There are words that have a long and bitter history, and often elicit associations that far outrun the intentions of those who employ them. It is my conviction that the term "betrayal" is such a word. Lest there be the slightest misunderstanding, I do not accuse Ellis of anti-Semitism, unintentional or intentional. His writings involve a different problem: he is largely indebted to the Christian liberation theologians for his theological framework. Unfortunately, their views of Jews and Judaism are almost uniformly shaped by the supersessionist theological claims of the church over the synagogue, as Ellis himself points out and against which he protests.

As is obvious from a reading of their works, the more prominent liberation theologians are far more at home in contemporary European social thought than they are with recent critical studies of first-century Christianity and Judaism. The presence of theological bias and the absence of critical, historical examination of the sources of first-century Judaism on the part of the liberation theologians is evident in their treatment of Jesus and the Pharisees. An appreciative summary of these views is offered by Dan Cohn-Sherbok. According to him, liberation theology offers Jews a "new orientation to Jesus."[4] In this perspective, the historical context of the Gospels is allegedly reclaimed for Christians and the primary emphasis falls on the "flesh and blood Jesus of history" rather than on the incarnate Lord of traditional theology.[5] As an example of this "new" perspective, Cohn-Sherbok writes: "The ancient prophets condemned the leaders of the nation; Jesus attacked the Scribes and Pharisees for their iniquity." Cohn-Sherbok then proceeds to list the "iniquities" of the Pharisees. They include "mockery of God's law," fostering of "moribund religious practices," and indifference to hunger so long as the Sabbath rituals were formally observed. Cohn-Sherbok quotes Juan L. Segundo on Jesus and the Pharisees: "The ultimate criterion in Jesus' theology is the remedy brought to some sort of human suffering."[6] Commenting on Segundo, Cohn-Sherbok writes, "The Pharisees did not share his concern; they were, in Jesus' words, a 'brood of vipers.' 'How can you speak good,' he asks, 'when you are evil?' "[7] Cohn-Sherbok also depicts Jesus as confronting the Pharisees "who were described in Luke as 'lovers of money' and condemning them for preferring to serve mammon rather than God."[8]

The fact that the authors of the Gospel narratives depict Jesus as having hostile and polemic attitudes toward the Pharisees is not in dispute. Nevertheless, the consensus of modern critical scholarship, both Jewish and Christian, is that the Gospels can no longer be regarded as literal, eyewitness accounts of the events they depict. Instead, each of the Gospels is seen as having been written and edited in the spirit of one of the Christian communities that arose in the aftermath of the Judeo-Roman War of 66–70 C.E. Each of these communities was in some sense a religious rival of the Pharisees, who were in turn divided among themselves. Jesus' encounters with the Pharisees, as depicted in the Gospels, must be read in the light of these conflicts. Put differently, the Gospels cannot be taken uncritically as historical documents; they must be seen, at least by theologians, in the light of the religious and political imperatives of the communities in which they arose.

An enormous amount of critical scholarship, both Christian and Jewish, has given us a more accurate and complete picture of the Pharisees than is to be found in either the Gospel accounts or the uncritical repetition of those accounts by the liberation theologians.[9] This is especially important in view of the fact that all branches of modern Judaism regard themselves as the spiritual heirs of the Pharisees and none would accept a view of the Pharisees that depicts them as a "brood of vipers" steeped in iniquity. This cannot be the basis of theological dialogue.

I was so astonished by the uncritical depiction of Jesus and the Pharisees in Rabbi Cohn-Sherbok's book that I asked him whether he concurs in the views of the Pharisees offered in his book. It is difficult to tell whether the views expressed are those of Cohn-Sherbok or of the liberation theologians. He told me that they were the views of the liberation theologians.

While the liberation theologians hold Moses and the prophets in high esteem, their view of the founders of the Jewish religious mainstream is based upon the traditional, negative stereotypes of the Pharisees and rabbinic Judaism, which predominated in the Christian world before the era of interreligious dialogue and unbiased critical scholarship. Moreover, as Ellis points out, the liberation theologians have no place in their writings for *contemporary* Jews. At the very least, fruitful theological dialogue between religious Jews and liberation theologians requires that the latter at least acquaint themselves with Christian critical scholarship on first-century Judaism and Christianity.

Although Ellis recognizes something of the anti-Jewish theological bias in the writings of the liberation theologians, I believe the negative bias in those writings has had a greater influence on his interpretations of the contemporary Jewish situation than he recognizes. This is especially evident in his treatment of the encounters between Jews and such groups as the Palestinians and the American black community. Where others are inclined to see tragic conflict, Ellis is prepared to see Jewish "betrayal" of Jewish ideals.

There are many important issues dividing Jewish conservatives and the mainstream black leadership in the United States. These include conservative distrust of affirmative action programs, the generally pro-Arab position of black leadership, and the place of honor and influence accorded by black activists to the author of the most overt public praise of Hitler's extermination program uttered by any American religious leader since World War II, the Rev. Louis Farakhan.

The issue of affirmative action is one in which blacks and Jewish conservatives are strongly at odds. Nevertheless, there is nothing distinctively Jewish about middle-class white opposition to affirmative action. Those middle-class whites, both Jewish and Christian, who prefer strict adherence to the merit system in employment and school admissions see affirmative action as giving blacks a government-sponsored unfair advantage. They do not see why they should be penalized for previous generations' exploitation of blacks. By contrast, blacks see themselves as having been disadvantaged by a social structure from which *all* whites have derived benefit. They regard affirmative action as indispensable to creating the beginnings of genuine equality in America. Values and interests are honestly in conflict on this issue. Regrettably, Ellis turns an honest conflict of interests into an expression of moral failing by one of the parties to the conflict, insisting that "justice" is on the side of the blacks and that Jewish views constitute a "betrayal" of Jewish ideals. As in the other conflicts he examines, the side he almost always faults is Jewish.

Another complaint raised by Ellis against the mainstream of the Jewish community is that the "policies and alliances" of the Jewish community both in Israel and in North America "increasingly resemble those historically used to oppress our own people." These are said to include "continued subjugation of the West Bank and Gaza Palestinians," Israel's "relations" with South Africa, and military assistance to "the murderous governments" of Guatemala and El Salvador. Ellis also sees "betrayal" in American-Jewish neoconservatism. Ellis traces the alleged turn to political conservatism, on the part of the leadership of the American Jewish community, to the Holocaust, the "formative event" for contemporary Judaism. He cites the feeling of isolation and abandonment that the Jews of the world experienced at the time of the Holocaust. The passive complicity of the overwhelming majority of the peoples of Europe in the extermination project was in some ways harder to bear than the outright acts of the avowed enemy. Those survivors foolish enough to try to return to their old homes after the war were often subject to the harshest harassment and, in some parts of Poland, outright murder. Under the circumstances, it was hardly surprising that most Holocaust survivors wanted nothing so much as the chance to leave the European continent forever.

According to Ellis, Rabbi Yitzchak Greenberg's theological and religious response to the Holocaust is representative of the Jewish mainstream. Ellis also finds Greenberg's religious thinking highly problematic. Greenberg sees "the statement made by the infinitely suffering Divine Presence in Auschwitz" as a call to humanity to stop the Holocaust and for the Jewish people to rise to "a new, unprecedented level of covenantal responsibility." According to Greenberg, that call was finally answered with the creation of the state of Israel, for Greenberg and for many others, the decisive religious fact of post-Holocaust Jewry.[10] Greenberg insists that in the post-Holocaust era the survival of the Jewish people, without which there can be no Judaism, has become the foundation value.

As Ellis points out, Greenberg sees the Holocaust as symbolizing radical alienation from God and "immersion in nihilism." However, this negative experience is dialectically linked to the positive experience of the recovery of Jerusalem and the Western Wall, the site of the ancient Jerusalem temple. Jerusalem thus symbolizes "the presence of God and the continuation of the people." After the experience of extermination and utter abandonment at Auschwitz, Greenberg holds that it is absolutely imperative that the Jews of Israel cease to be victims and do whatever they must to insure their survival. Thus, achieving sufficient power to guarantee the survival of the state of Israel, insofar as such a guarantee is humanly possible, has been elevated by Greenberg to a sacred principle. In the post-Holocaust period, endangering that power becomes the closest thing to an unpardonable sin for Judaism. As Ellis points out, there is something close to unanimity on this point among the Holocaust theologians, among whom Ellis includes Emil L. Fackenheim and myself.

Ellis argues that Greenberg's elevation of power to a sacred principle is highly problematic, as Greenberg would himself acknowledge. Greenberg's position is not unlike the realism of Reinhold Niebuhr and seems to be derived from Max Weber's contrast between an "ethic of responsibility" and an "ethic of ultimate ends."[11] According to Greenberg, Israel's present exercise of power can no longer be judged in the light of the absolute standards of the ancient prophets. When Israel commits itself to action in the political sphere, guilt and imperfect responses are inevitable. Only the utterly powerless can judge political action in terms of absolute standards of good and evil. Following Nietzsche, I would add that the use of such standards by the powerless is an important psychological weapon in their own struggle for power. In place of an absolute standard of good and evil, Greenberg offers a pragmatism new to Jewish experience. Admittedly, such a pragmatism inevitably leads to the "occasional use of immoral strategies to achieve moral ends." To guard against abuse, Greenberg insists that the exercise of power must not be divorced from self-criticism and a sense of obligation and empathy toward the Palestinians. Nevertheless, under no circumstances can Israel grant any degree of empowerment to the Palestinians that would endanger the existence and security of the Jewish people.[12] To do so is, according to Greenberg, unintentionally to collaborate with attempted genocide.

It is at this point that Ellis's disagreement with Greenberg and the "Holocaust theologians" is most emphatic. Ellis sees the Holocaust theologians as representing the regnant ideology of the mainstream American Jewish community, an idea that cannot be said to be true of my version of Holocaust theology. Ellis argues that the Jewish community has opted for power in place of powerlessness, and that the price of that fundamental choice "now seems prohibitive." Among the negative expressions of "empowerment" Ellis includes: "The rise of the neoconservative movement in North America" and "the ascendancy to power in Israel of religious and secular expansionists, exemplified by Rabbi Meir Kahane . . . and Ariel Sharon." Ellis further argues that the Jewish community, presumably the

Israeli community, has exchanged the misery of the victim for the role of "conqueror." He accuses the Jewish community of having forgotten its own oppression and having opened "the possibility of becoming an oppressor."

Ellis cites approvingly the harsh judgments leveled at Jewish neoconservatives by Earl Shorris and Roberta Strauss Feuerlicht. Shorris contends that Jewish neoconservatives oppose helping blacks or other minorities because the blacks are anti-Semitic and the others will become so. Shorris also argues that the neoconservatives hold that the state of Israel can do no wrong, the Palestinians have no right to a state, the killing of an Israeli civilian by a Palestinian is an act of terror whereas the killing of a Palestinian civilian by an Israeli is an act of self-defense. Moreover, Shorris assigns to the Jews the view that the poor in America are an underclass without dignity that can best be served by neglect since only through the goad of necessity will the poor ever achieve a dignified place in American life.[13] Regrettably, Shorris offers a malicious caricature of responsible conservative opinion rather than an accurate account. No responsible conservative holds that the state of Israel can do no wrong. Nor do conservatives take issue with black leadership because of the latter's alleged anti-Semitism but because of honest differences on issues, some of which are discussed above. That terrorism has been practiced by both sides in the Arab-Israeli conflict cannot be denied. Nor is there any doubt that innocent Palestinans have been killed both before and during the *intifada*. Nevertheless, Shorris's equation of the cold-blooded killing of the innocent of all ages, both Jewish and non-Jewish, on land, sea, and in the air by Arab terrorists with the behavior of the Israeli army and even hard-line Israeli settlers toward the Palestinians is beneath contempt, as is his statement that the poor are regarded by Jewish conservatives as an underclass without dignity. It would obviously be best for both the Israelis and the Palestinians were it possible for the Palestinians to have a state of their own *without endangering Israel's existence*. It is, however, worth remembering that a state is the institution that has a monopoly on the legitimate use of instruments of power and coercion within a given territory. Before the Israelis consent to such a transfer of power, they had better have realistic assurance that the guns of the newly established Palestinian state are not ultimately used against them. It is regrettable that Ellis has chosen to take Shorris seriously.

Ellis also approves of the views of Roberta Strauss Feuerlicht who argues that all Jews are bound together not by statehood but by "the burden they placed upon themselves and posterity when they internalized morality and gave the world the ethical imperative."[14] Having defined the bond allegedly uniting Jewry, Feuerlicht proceeds to accuse the Jews of violating their own ethical imperatives. She condemns them for having been "slave owners, slave traders, and slave auctioneers" out of all proportion to their numbers in the antebellum south. This is a rather curious accusation and one wonders what Feuerlicht's motives were for making it. The ancestors of the vast majority of American Jews did not arrive in the United States until after the Civil War. Moreover, in the antebellum period the majority did not live in the south. Yet Feuerlicht feels compelled to impute to "the Jews" the bearing of the guilt of slavery as an institution. Clearly, Feuerlicht is more interested in establishing the so-called guilt of contemporary Jews vis-à-vis the blacks than in establishing a genuine past grievance. Although Feuerlicht admits that many Jews participated in the civil rights movement of the 1960s, she characterizes the current position of the Jewish community toward the blacks as bordering on arrogance.

Feuerlicht sees the state of Israel as founded upon a policy of expropriation and denial of the rights of Palestinians. She therefore condemns the state of Israel as an example of colonialism rather than national liberation. Feuerlicht nevertheless concedes that the state of Israel must continue to exist because the alternative would be another Holocaust.

Ellis concludes his discussion of Shorris and Feuerlicht by suggesting that they have assumed the role of latter-day prophets in the Jewish community. Ellis sees the contemporary prophet as critiquing Israel's sale of arms to right-wing governments in Central America, Israel's "continuing contributions to the scientific, military, and economic interests of South Africa," and its "wholesale expropriation of Palestinian land on the West Bank and in Gaza." He sees Shorris and Feuerlicht as naming the "new forms of idolatry" embraced by the Jewish community: "capitalism; nationalism; survival at any cost." I return to Ellis's treatment of the issue of Jewish survival below.

In spite of what he considers the failings of the American and Israeli Jewish mainstreams, Ellis is somewhat encouraged by "movements of Jewish renewal." In almost every instance, the political agenda of these movements is on the left. They include the New Jewish Agenda in the United States, the Oz VeShalom movement in Israel, which strongly opposes continued Israeli occupation of the West Bank and Gaza, and the Jewish peace movement. Ellis is especially encouraged by the action of Todd Kaplan, who was part of a group who entered the Martin Marietta plant in Orlando, Florida, in April 1984 and used hammers to damage several of the Army's Pershing II intermediate-range ballistic missiles, which were being fabricated at the plant. The group also poured blood on the installation. While this was going on, Kaplan blew a shofar as a symbolic call to repentance. Kaplan characterized the event as the "Plowshares action." He was subsequently sentenced to a three-year term in the minimum security federal prison in Danbury, Connecticut.

Ellis characterizes Kaplan's behavior as an "act for justice." He cites with approval Kaplan's defense of the "Plowshares action":

I believe that the elimination of nuclear arms is a goal we Jews should embrace. . . . We should take the idea of holocaust prevention both seriously and personally. . . . There is a risk in not doing anything, especially in preventing . . . nuclear wars. And that is really why I went and did the Plowshares action. I believe it is "holocaust prevention" in the purest sense. This is an act that is possible before it's too late, before our whole planet becomes one huge death camp.

Ellis's use of Kaplan's "Plowshares action" highlights the profound difference between his political theology and a more conservative political theology. Kaplan characterizes his action as "Holocaust prevention," but the Holocaust he has in mind is a nuclear Holocaust. He appears to believe that the unilateral destruction of American nuclear weapons, whether by acts of civil disobedience such as his or by government decision, will somehow diminish the possibility of a nuclear Holocaust. Nowhere in his book does Ellis consider the voluminous literature on the subject of arms control, disarmament, and deterrence that has developed since 1945.

Kaplan's theatrical behavior is utterly unrelated to the real world of nuclear weapons. The United States and the Soviet Union have avoided the ultimate horror of nuclear warfare for over forty years. As is well known, the superiority of the Soviet Union and the Warsaw pact nations in conventional armaments has been balanced by the nuclear arsenal possessed by the United States, Britain, and France. When a realistic opportunity arose for both sides to reduce nuclear weapons, the conservative, anticommunist administration of Ronald Reagan took the steps necessary to do so. That process is still going on. The dramatic changes that have taken place under President Mikhael Gorbachev are likely to lead to further reductions. To the extent that the danger of nuclear war has been reduced, it has not been as a result of the irresponsible theatrics of men and women like Todd Kaplan, but by the hard, deliberate labor of experts on both sides who have weighed the consequences of all the likely scenarios and found a credible way to begin arms reduction. These observations are in no sense meant to diminish the contribution of the peace movement to the process. Still, members of the peace movement have been most effective when they have weighed the realistic political and military consequences of the moves they have proposed.

Ellis faults the Holocaust theologians for having "virtually nothing to say about the ethics of a Jewish state possessing nuclear weapons." For Ellis mere possession of such weapons is an evil. Although the Israelis have never admitted that they possess a nuclear arsenal, there is wide agreement among arms control experts that Israel does in fact possess such weapons. Israel's policy has been characterized as that of a "bomb in the basement," meaning that the Israelis have the bomb but find it prudent to refrain from going public.[15]

Nowhere does Ellis discuss Israel's reasons for believing that it must possess a nuclear arsenal. Similarly, in discussing Israel's occupation of the West Bank and Gaza, Ellis is more concerned with the hurt done to Palestinians than with the reasons most Israelis feel they have no choice but to hold on to the occupied territories, in spite of the harm done both to

Palestinian and Israeli society by the occupation. Ellis complains that Holocaust theology is unable to articulate a path of solidarity with the Palestinian people. He further asserts that an essential task of Jewish theology must be to "deabsolutize" the state of Israel. Regrettably, Ellis has little to say concerning the refusal of the Arab states, save Egypt, to make peace with Israel in over forty years, their persistent attempts to delegitimize Israel by the obscene Zionism-is-racism U.N. resolution and their oft-repeated statement, uttered more often in Arabic than in English, that their ultimate goal is to destroy the state of Israel. Nor when discussing the occupation does Ellis mention the fact that the West Bank was occupied because Jordan went to war against Israel in 1967 and was soundly defeated in spite of entreaties by the Israeli government that it remain out of the conflict. Having lost the war, Jordan never sought to make peace with Israel. It is one thing for Israel to give up territory to an enemy who is willing to enter into a credible peace treaty. It is an altogether different matter to give up a territorial buffer to enemies bent on destruction.

Few Jews like to see Israeli soldiers beating up Palestinians or blowing up their houses. Moreover, Israeli policy toward the Palestinians has had its share of errors, misperceptions, and miscalculations. Nevertheless, the real problem is that neither the Palestinians nor the Israelis see the Palestinians of the West Bank and Gaza as powerless or Israel as powerful as does Ellis. In spite of Ellis's constant references to the heavy moral price the Jews are paying for "empowerment," the Palestinians see themselves as part of the larger Arab world that will some day overwhelm and destroy the Israelis as an earlier generation of Arabs destroyed the crusader kingdoms. Both sides understand that the Arabs can sustain innumerable defeats without having any incentive to make peace. They are convinced that sooner or later they will win the final war.

In spite of Ellis's insistence that the lessons of the Holocaust are largely irrelevant to Israel's current situation of what he strangely calls "empowerment," and his contention that Holocaust theology is irrelevant to the situation in contemporary Israel, *the Holocaust is precisely the operative model the Israelis must consider as their worst possible case scenario.* The Holocaust cannot be used as a model for day-to-day relations between Jews and non-Jews, either in the Diaspora or even in the encounter between Israeli and Palestinian. Nevertheless, few military analysts have any doubt that a decisive defeat of Israel by the Palestinians and the Arab states would be followed by a merciless slaughter that would assure the Arabs of the "final solution" of their Jewish problem. Robert Harkavy has succinctly stated the reasons why the Arabs will be satisfied with nothing less than total vengeance:

The Middle East conflict is not fundamentally one of territorial irredentism or self-determination, nor is it simply a zero-sum clash of rival nationalisms over control of Palestine. These are contributing factors. A more fundamental reason that a permanent peace is virtually impossible is the overwhelming, deepseated humiliation felt by all Arabs over having been defeated six times in wars by Israel.[16]

Both the Holocaust and the consistently antagonist positions taken against Israel in the United Nations provide a realistic basis for assessing the kind of help Israel might expect from any of the nations of the world if it were ever threatened with imminent extermination. On the contrary, in such a case there is every likelihood that many foreign offices even in the Western world would regard the Arab action as a convenient exercise in problem-solving.

Ellis argues that "at the center of the struggle to be faithful as a Jew today is the suffering and liberation of the Palestinian people." Furthermore, he requires "a fundamental confession and repentance of past and present transgressions" on the part of the Jews. Thus, for Ellis the weight of solving the conflict is thrust upon the Israelis with little or no consideration of the persistent Palestinian inability (or refusal) to offer their own *credible* scenario in which Israeli-Palestinian coexistence might be possible. In contrast to those Israeli fundamentalists who see Israel's claim to the whole of Palestine and even Jordan as divinely mandated, I believe that the optimum solution to the Arab-Israeli conflict would be one in which the national aspirations of both communities are reasonably satisfied. Unfortunately, the PLO made a promise to the Jews that after Hitler can neither be forgotten nor explained away—the promise to drive the Jews out of the land and into the seas. Since making that threat Yassir Arafat has moderated his position in a number of ambiguous revisions of the original Palestinian intent, the revisions having a different meaning and intent depending upon whether they were expressed in a Western language or in Arabic. Nevertheless, once having been uttered, the promise to destroy Israel is one promise that no Jew can dismiss after the Holocaust. It was Elie Wiesel who wrote in his novel *Night* that only Hitler kept his promises to the Jews. In the aftermath of Hitler, Jews are no longer disposed to ignore such promises. When the Israelis look at the *intifada,* they do not see a Palestinian population seeking to create a national existence alongside of them. They see a population determined to take the necessary steps eventually to destroy them.

Ellis raises the problem of justice for the Palestinians. However, justice is not an abstract concept but one rooted in the realities of communal living. One owes very little to those who are pledged to destroy one's community. Words about Israeli-Palestinian solidarity come easily, but there can be no solidarity when both sides have reason to believe, as many of them do, that they are locked in long-term mortal combat. As Ellis recognizes, the Holocaust made the creation of the state of Israel absolutely imperative. The European Jewish community was finished. With the birth of the state of Israel, the Jews were brutally expelled from Arab lands, a population "solution" only the most extremist Israelis propose for the Palestinians. The ingathering of the exiles was neither an act of colonialism/imperialism nor a felicitous act of voluntary homecoming, but the desperate act of people for whom the world offered no other place. Surrounded on all sides by enemies who regard it as a wholly alien presence destined sooner or later to be destroyed as were the crusader kingdoms, founded in the aftermath of the extermination of Europe's Jews, the state of Israel has created a nuclear arsenal as a deterrent against its own destruction. *Israel's basic nuclear strategy consists in radically escalating the cost of exterminating its citizens.* This strategy is largely a consequence of the destruction of Europe's Jews during World War II. It was also a consequence of the expulsion of the Jews from Muslim lands. The Israelis know that, at its most merciful, an Arab victory over Israel would result in yet another total expulsion. In Nazi Europe the victims lacked all means of self-defense and were incapable of inflicting significant damage on their enemies. There was little, if any, economic cost to the Germans in the extermination project when the value of confiscated Jewish property and the use of Jewish institutions to facilitate the destruction is factored in.[17] In a future conflict, an Israeli resort to nuclear weapons would, of course, be utterly suicidal. Nevertheless, after the Germans succeeded in slaughtering millions of Jews with impunity, and after the Arabs promised to do the same to the Israelis, it is highly unlikely that the Israelis would go silently into the dust. Israel's deterrent strategy can be seen as a variation on the MAD strategy, mutually assured destruction.

Methodologically, Ellis is entirely consistent in seeking to diminish the relevance of Holocaust theology and of the Holocaust for the contemporary Jewish situation. Instead of garnering the exceedingly modest resources of the post-Holocaust Jewish community to assure its own survival, Ellis demands that Jews adopt the utopian program of moving "beyond empowerment to a liberation encompassing *all those struggling for justice,* including those we *once* knew as enemy" (italics added). Apart from the fact that few, if any, of the larger and more powerful peoples of the world have adopted a program of justice for all people save as pious rhetoric, it does not seem to have occurred to Ellis that in a world of conflicting peoples with conflicting rights, it is utterly impossible to render justice to all. That is why theologians, both Christian and Jewish, cannot entirely ignore the doctrine of the Fall. Moreover, Ellis's call for a deabsolutizing Israel seems to anticipate Israel's eventual demise. Ellis argues that it might be possible for Israel to avoid defeat and annihilation by making "peace when you are powerful." Here again, Ellis *prefers the utopian to the actual.* Apart from the fact that Israel is not powerful in any realistic, long-term sense, Ellis's proposal that Israel seek peace makes sense only if there were someone with whom to make peace. To expect that the Palestinians would be satisfied with a rump state on the West Bank and in Gaza is contrary to all we know about their national aspirations and their sense of national dignity.

Even that much would seriously threaten Israel at a time when Arab wealth, numbers, and technological sophistication continue to increase.

Ellis recognizes that military defeat may someday come to Israel. Here again, he is compelled to devalue the Holocaust as a model for the outcome of such a defeat:

> But if military defeat does come and if the civilian population is attacked, the result, though tragic, will not by any meaningful definition be another Holocaust. And it would not, by any means, signal the end of the Jewish people, as many Holocaust theologians continue to speculate.

No person can accurately predict the future. Ellis may be correct in his optimism concerning a military defeat, but no responsible Jewish leader dare risk a situation in which the lives of Israel's Jews depend upon the tender mercies of the Palestinians or their fellow Arabs. Nor would the mortal threat be faced solely by the Israelis. As Robert Harkavy has argued, "levels of anti-Semitism would rise rather than fall if Israel were destroyed and its people massacred" for "there has been a historical psychological connection between Jewish defeat . . . and sadistic anti-Semitism."[18]

Ellis's theological views are important because they are an authentic expression of what a *Jewish version of Christian liberation theology* would be like. By contrast, a genuinely *Jewish liberation theology* would take greater account of recent and current Jewish history. In particular, that which Ellis so readily denounces as oppression and betrayal, a Jewish liberation theology would understand as tragic conflict. As with a nonutopian Christian theology, it would work for the realistic amelioration of the inhuman condition of the marginalized. It would do so by soundly-based economic and political measures that take full account of the modernizing economic and technological forces that have fostered mass marginalization since the beginnings of the industrial revolution.[19] It would under no circumstances seek an overturning of the current economic and political order, which would inevitably end in tyranny, mass repression, and mass murder by regimes far more inhuman than the present bourgeois or rightwing governments, as the history of both the Soviet Union and the Peoples Republic of China demonstrate. Above all, such a theology would insist that the Holocaust has lost none of its relevance for Jewish faith and experience. On the contrary, in spite of fantasies of Jewish empowerment the Holocaust gains further relevance with the *intifada* as an ever-present reminder of the fate that awaits Israel should its defenses ever falter.

NOTES

1. Marc H. Ellis, *Toward a Jewish Theology of Liberation*, 2nd ed. (Maryknoll, N.Y.: Orbis Books, 1989) and Dan Cohn-Sherbok, *On Earth as It Is in Heaven: Jews,*

Christians, and Liberation Theology (Maryknoll, N.Y.: Orbis Books, 1987).

2. I am indebted to Helen Fein, *Accounting for Genocide* (New York: Free Press, 1979), for this concept.

3. See Richard L. Rubenstein, *After Auschwitz* (Indianapolis: Bobbs-Merrill, 1966), pp. 30–31.

4. Cohn-Sherbok, *On Earth*, p. 35.

5. Ibid.

6. Juan L. Segundo, *The Liberation of Theology* (Maryknoll, N.Y.: Orbis Books, 1976), p. 79.

7. Cohn-Sherbok, *On Earth*, p. 43.

8. Ibid., pp. 45-46.

9. A good place to begin is Jacob Neusner, *From Politics to Piety: The Emergence of Pharisaic Judaism* (Englewood Cliffs, N.J.: Prentice-Hall, 1973).

10. Irving Greenberg, "The Third Great Cycle in Jewish History," *Perspectives* (National Jewish Resource Center, 1981), p. 18.

11. This distinction is discussed in Max Weber, "Politics as a Vocation," in H. H. Gerth and C. Wright Mills, *From Max Weber: Essays in Sociology* (New York: Oxford University Press, 1946).

12. Greenberg, "Third Great Cycle," pp. 25–26.

13. These views are expressed in Robert Shorris, *Jews Without Mercy: A Lament* (Garden City, N.Y.: Doubleday, 1982).

14. Roberta Strauss Feuerlicht, *The Fate of the Jews: A People Torn Between Israeli Power and Jewish Ethics* (New York: Times Books, 1983), p. 31.

15. On the subject of Israel's ambiguous statements concerning the possibility that it possesses nuclear weapons, see Alan Dowtry, "Going Public with the Bomb," in *Transaction: Social Science and Modern Society*, pp. 52–58.

16. Robert Harkavy, "Survival Imperatives," *Transaction: Social Science and Modern Society* (January/February 1986), p. 63. Harkavy's article contains an excellent discussion of the reasons why Israel's survival requires a nuclear deterrent.

17. This subject is discussed by Helen Fein, *Accounting for Genocide*.

18. Harkavy, "Survival Imperatives," p. 64.

19. I have addressed that issue in detail in Richard L. Rubenstein, *The Age of Triage* (Boston: Beacon Press, 1983).

9

God's Pain and Our Pain

How Theology Has To Change after Auschwitz

DOROTHEE SÖLLE

Elie Wiesel described in a play the trial of Schamgorod. It is set in Russia at the time of the Chmielnik pogrom, in which one hundred thousand Jews were sacrificed. Following an old tradition a Purim play is performed in a small village inn at Schamgorod: three Purim actors act out a trial in which God is accused of allowing children to suffer. The play takes place after a pogrom. While the actors drink and celebrate the feast with the traditional freedom of speech, which allows things to be said that otherwise no one would dare to say, outside the murderous bands are again coming together. Strictly speaking, the play takes place in the short interval between two pogroms and deals with the theme of theodicy. In vain the three drunken Purim actors attempt to find someone to defend God. The plaintiff says:

No counsel for the defense, so what?! Whose fault is that then? He has killed his defenders, delivered them to the murderers. He didn't spare Reb Schmouel, the judge. He didn't save the life of Reb Baruch, the teacher. Wise Hirsch and Meilech the shoemaker, loved him and believed in him, in him alone, and he didn't care about them at all. . . . Whose fault is it then if they are silent? Whose fault is it if they have turned to dust? Whose fault is it if the earth is populated with murderers — and only with murderers?[1]

Toward the end of the play a stranger appears out of the night, a beautiful and cold twilight figure named Sam. He is prepared to play the defending counsel for God. He protests the omnipotence and absoluteness of God. "I am his servant. He created the world and us without seeking our opinion.

He can act as he pleases. Our task is to glorify him notwithstanding."[2] As the players all put on their masks to begin the play at last, Sam dons the mask of the devil, breaks out into long, loud laughter, and makes a sign toward the outside. The door bursts open and the pack rushes in.

I think that this play takes the theme of theodicy more seriously than does traditional theology, which so often remains in the position of the defender. The seriousness is expressed in the highly fickle and comic manner in which the roles are allocated: the three drunken Purim actors are the judges; the innkeeper's daughter, who lost her sanity after a gang rape, is witness for the prosecution; the old innkeeper, the most religious, is the inexorable plaintiff. The defendant is, "as is his wont," as is said ironically at one point, absent. And the adroit theologian, who defends God, turns out to be the devil. He calls himself the "messenger of God. I rove over the earth and report to him. I see everything, know everything. It is true that I can create nothing, but I can destroy everything."[3]

Accusation and defense, evidence and court represent an intellectual model, in which the leap into the next metaphysical level is precluded: this is the strength of the playwright, Elie Wiesel. He does not allow the question to be neutralized or historicized. If we have to accuse God, can we defend God? Is there a defense that God is not satanic, but based on a greater love? Or is accusing God the greatest gesture of love for God that we can make, as it appears in many of Wiesel's characters? We theologians, who should tell of God's deeds and praise God's being, where do we belong in this play? What has Christian theology in particular to say today?

I pose this question after Auschwitz. I cannot and will not set it outside time. I cannot compare the Lisbon earthquake of 1755 with the Holocaust of the Jews by the Germans. My question concerns Christian theology. Which points must be modified and what direction must it take after the Shoah?

This question leads to a critical rereading of the New Testament and its anti-Jewish tendencies. It leads also to a rewrite of church history with regard to the relationship of Christianity to Judaism over the ages. It also has consequences for systematic theological thought and compels us to revise our comprehension of God, as I wish to discuss in this essay.

The form of response developed in the West to the question of suffering has become theodicy. I suspect that fixing on the problem of theodicy is a way of avoiding or denying suffering. If we solve the problem with a justification of God as regards the suffering of the innocent, then we deny it in the classic masculine theological manner. But there is also a post-Christian philosophical denial, which proceeds on a historical basis. This entails the application of a century in the history of philosophy to the problem. The history of the problem of theodicy in philosophy is the history of "progressive distancing from or retraction of a totalitarianism or monopoly of interpretation," corresponding to "an increasing narrowing of concepts such as rationality, discursiveness, and consistency."[4] Right up to modern times the "ancient European theory of harmony" remains valid, "according to which God and also nature do not allow the existence of pure suffering and evil."

Ideological continuity, such an important historical perception from the history of philosophy, makes theodicy not—yet—necessary. Where the commitment to schemes of religious interpretation "has completely disintegrated, theodicy is equally no [longer] necessary—and also no longer possible."[5]

Under this interpretation of history—seen from a European and inherently Christian point of view—God has had many defenders for some time, but today accusation and defense have become unnecessary. Even the Holocaust does not urge this kind of secular thought to conclusions that upset our own clear horizon. One has, so to speak, always known that God is irrelevant. Auschwitz adds nothing to this knowledge. I suspect that one of the reasons for this change of paradigm achieved in the German theory of history, in which Hitler's action was termed "Asiatic," and the history of Stalin's crime is made to bear the brunt in order to trivialize the German crime, is a consequent freedom of religion. Certain questions are no longer posed both from the perspective of the victim and from that of the perpetrator: suffering and guilt are by necessity made even by being compared on a historical basis. The other point of difficulty, for which the word "God" is still used, is leveled. In Niklas Luhmann's theoretical system, for example, the meaning of reflection dwindles to the function of meditation and the interpretation of "the collective given meaning."[6]

In the technological age, reason no longer has any identity in the emphatic sense, because it is limited to a "harmony (of the feelings, social groups, economic contrasts), even if only in the foreground" and in a certain sense represents not only the "postmodern" end of the still religiously motivated modern philosophy, but also the coming to an end of the philosophy that was still related to general reason. For technological, instrumental reason, "the question of suffering and evil is dropped from the field of philosophy and [is] referred back to those who evidently can no longer comfort mankind."[7] The practical application of this type of philosophy is today so-called acceptance research, which is used to establish how much encumbrance and disturbance of life the imperium can impose in a particular region. Acceptance replaces theodicy!

What does this historical backward glance mean for a system of theological thought?

In a relatively short period of the history of Western philosophy, the proponents of theodicy have attempted to reconcile three qualities of God: omnipotence, love, and intelligibility. The result of the debate can be summarized in that only two of these three theologumena are conceivable at any one time, while the remaining one must always be excluded.

The first position is that God is omnipotent and intelligible. God stands, metaphorically speaking, at the head of the universe as the great disposer, the organizer, the one who is really responsible; as the one who can step in and end the torment of humankind, assuming, of course, that God wishes to. In this context we often speak of the suffering of the innocent, of children, for example, who are tortured. But in a deeper sense all people are innocent. No one deserves to starve and of the six million gassed, not one of them ever, even if a liar or thief, "deserved" the suffering that was inflicted on them.

An omnipotent God, who imposes suffering, who benignly looks down on Auschwitz from above, must be a sadist. That kind of God stands on the side of the victors, and is, in the words of a black American theologian, "a white racist."[8] This is the position of Satan in Wiesel's play: he always appears where murder is committed. He is the advocate of submission. His God is pure power. And a theology that conceives of such a supreme ruler, organizer, responsible provoker and creator, reflects the sadism of those who invented it.

The second position conceives of God indeed as omnipotent and all-loving, but at the same time as unintelligible God eludes us. Belief in God becomes absurd or, at best, a paradox. "I lost my belief in God at Verdun" is a well-known expression of mass atheism. If God has become completely unintelligible, God can no longer be held fast to in the long term, even in paradoxical belief.

What does this tenet from the First World War mean for the things that happened after? I suspect that after Auschwitz, from the point of view of the Germans (for whom alone I can speak here), nothing like this was said, not only because God had long been forgotten, but also because the element of guilt, even if not confessed to, makes the innocence of the first tenet impossible. In view of the Holocaust I cannot talk simply of "losing" God: chance participation compels one to other forms of speaking of God and must thus lead beyond the omnipotent all-loving God.

The third position conceives of God as love, but not as omnipotent. Between the victors and the victims, God is credible only if God is on the side of the victims, if God is thought capable of suffering. This position is represented today by such different Jewish philosophers as Elie Wiesel, Abraham Heschel, and Hans Jonas, but also by a popular theologian such as Rabbi Kuschner.[9] On the Christian side I can name, above all, Dietrich Bonhoeffer, who became increasingly close to the suffering God while in prison. I can also mention litigation theology, which articulates God's indigence and growth, and I can mention the theology of liberation, both in its Latin American and in its feminist forms.

In the following I wish to think of the suffering godhead, which is the only possible response to the question of the suffering of the innocent. I do not wish to respond to the question of theodicy, but to show it to be a false question. The religious question of suffering is no longer the one so often heard: How can God permit that?, but a more difficult one, which first has to be studied: How does our pain become God's pain and how does God's pain appear in our pain? In speaking of "God's pain," I am liberating myself from the compulsory concepts of the patriarchs: God as dictator, God at the head of hierarchical thought, God as omnipotent—I find these theological notions of the patriarchs distasteful and despicable. And an unchanging, eternal God, who is utterly self-sufficient and beyond need and vulnerability cannot, or, at least, can only cynically, answer the question of human suffering. Such a God must be prosecuted and our desire to defend God disappears. Under the spiritual terms of the patriarchs, under the theology of the omnipotent God, the argument about theodicy is still the best that can emerge. In attempting to introduce God's pain, I am setting this false concept right. I am not speaking of anything that God could avoid or abolish. When we speak of the pain of God, then we no longer see God in a purely masculine presentation. God is then our mother who cries about what we do to each other and about what we brothers and sisters do to animals and plants. God consoles us as a mother does, she cannot wave away pain magically (although that occasionally happens!), but she holds us on her lap, sometimes until we stand up again, our strength renewed, sometimes in a darkness without light. To call this darkness the "darkness of God," to be able to call it this, is the real difficulty of a theological discussion after the Holocaust: not to yield this darkness to an anti-God, to a different, dualistically opposed, principle, that is *the* challenge of theology after Auschwitz.

God cannot comfort us if she were not bound to us in pain, if she did not have this wonderful and exceptional ability to feel the pain of another in her own body, suffering with us, existing with us. I shall attempt to show how this theology of pain derives from Christian tradition.

The evangelists describe Jesus as someone who has this ability. If someone's face is slapped in his presence, he winces and feels it on his own cheek. If someone is lied to in his presence, he too wants the truth. If a whole nation is suppressed under the brutal force of imperialism, he weeps over his Jerusalem.

The words I have said, "if in his presence," have physical limitations. Let us now try to think of God and remove this limitation. All those who suffer are in the presence of God. There is no "if" anymore. God does not forget. The *praesentia Dei* is never simply an observing presence, but always the pain or joy of God. Without the pain of God, God is not really present, but simply appearing, like a president does when occasionally visiting the people. But God participates in the suffering of people. God is here and suffered with us. Truly? In each suffering, each injured vanity, each toothache, each frustration that life inflicts on us? I think that before we can consider God's pain and our pain together, we must first learn to differentiate them. The New Testament is very clear on this point. Paul distinguishes in the Second Letter to the Corinthians between "worldly grief" and "godly grief" (2 Cor. 7:10). He says of worldly grief that it produces death. It knows no hope, it leads to nothing. When I think of "worldly grief," I think of the terrible illnesses of prosperity, such as alcoholism, anorexia, workaholism, to name but a few. These illnesses occur in a climate of prosperity, which ignores our nonmaterial needs and manipulates them in such a way that they are transformed into addictions. People become the victims of an apparently rich, orderly world, and transfer to their body and their soul the terrible disorder and the spiritual poverty of the whole.

Paul compares this "worldly grief" to a different kind: "For godly grief produces a repentance that leads to salvation and brings no regret, but worldly grief produces death" (2 Cor. 7:10). What is this "affliction wished by God"? This different pain, which does not go round in circles, but also brings about complete change? How do we differentiate our pain, which so often only expresses worldly grief, from the pain of God?

The answer of an atheistic consumer culture to the question of suffering is "Get rid of it! Take the pill! And preferably straightaway!" Suffering is pushed to one side like an irksome shadow. In this style of life, the human being is considered like a machine: it functions, it produces, it goes or it is out of action; it does not work anymore and must be completely replaced or have new parts. This model of the technological machine rules our way of thinking. The machine does not feel pain. There are also theologians who appear to me to represent God as a great indestructible machine. It continues to function presumably even after nuclear war and the destruction of creation.

For this theology it makes no difference whether it arose before or after Auschwitz. God's transcendence has been dissociated from God's immanence, even if the claim continues to be made that in theory they both support each other. In such fantasies of God I see indeed the power, the greatness, the independence of God perfectly expressed, but I cannot find in this concept any hint of the pain of God or of the bond of God. I therefore find it difficult to believe in the love of God within such a concept. The totally transcendent God is not bound with us in pain, but Paul's distinction between worldly grief and the godly grief (*lypa kata theon*) then loses its meaning if there is no grief in God.

In the context of Paul's letters, affliction mostly means the adversities befalling the apostle as the proclaimer of deliverance: the chicanery of authorities, prison, threats to his life, torture, death. Paul attributes to both types of grief, worldly grief and that of God, the results they produce. Godly grief results from the pain of God at a barbaric world filled with injustice and the destruction of life. To participate in this pain of God is to perceive God's grief. "You have understood its meaning. What zeal it has aroused in you! You offered resistance! You were indignant and alarmed, you desired change, you forced it to happen and you called the guilty to account" (2 Cor. 7:11) according to J. Zink. We must read Paul's letters as documents of resistance to the Roman Empire, which resulted from belief in Christ the liberator. Within grief wished by God, are contained: to be alarmed, to offer resistance, to desire change and to force it to happen, and to call the guilty to account. This grief does not go round in circles, it does not brood within itself. It is a grief such as we find in our hearts against the extirpation of creation and the pillaging of the poor. It is the grief present in Martin Luther King, Jr., and in Dag Hammarskjöld, the horror that can never be abated at the brutality of a system that wants to function but does not share in the pain of God and does not admit the vulnerability of God.

In the Gospel of John also, whose anti-Judaism I will not go into here, the situation of the Christian community is understood to be one of persecution in the Roman Empire. The Christians in this small community in Palestine at the end of the first century have lived their day-to-day lives in a prison of fear; the word "world" no longer retains here the meaning it had in ancient Greece of cosmos, order, ornament, and beauty, but rather expresses enmity to God, a world full of dangers and falsehood, a world that God hates, which destroys light and life, and in which the community is afraid. "In the world you have tribulation" (John 16:33). Life is hopeless, and perhaps Mary Magdalene, in continuing to weep and refusing to be consoled over the murder of Jesus, is the clearest witness for the pain that fixed the minority of the Christians in their perception of life in this world of persecution and triumphant injustice. Mary Magdalene does not accuse God, she does not defend God, she weeps; she is too deep in God to allow accusation or self-defense. Accusation would have required distance from God and she would have run away like the male disciples. But she is in God's pain. "Truly, truly, I say to you," says the Christ of John, "you will weep and lament, but the world will rejoice" (John 16:20). Those who rejoice are those who celebrate the triumphal processions of the Roman emperors when a small nation is again forced to its knees, ravaged, pillaged, and sold into slavery. The world will rejoice—this refers to the splendid gladiator fights and sports shows that the Romans held to distract from the misery of hunger. "You will weep and lament," because in a world of legitimized force, each word that speaks seriously of justice and peace is beaten down and scorned. The Romans knew precisely what threat the Christian communities posed for the politico-religious state consensus.

A recent visit to El Salvador has helped me to a better understanding of the New Testament. In this tiny country, under the heel of the imperium, the poor weep and lament when their crops are burnt, and when their teachers and trade unionists are dragged away and made to disappear. When, under Decree No. 50, the secret services and security forces are free to torture all prisoners for fourteen days as they wish, "you will weep, but the world will rejoice." At the same time the television, firmly in the hands of the imperium and their local collaborators, shows sport and fashion shows. Each day $1.5 million flow into this tiny land, chiefly as military aid, supposedly for liberation, but in actuality for the ever-continuing "low-intensity warfare." More than one million dollars each day for napalm and electrical torturing devices, for low-level flights that force the people to flee, for watchtowers and barbed wire, for army boots and blood.

God's pain and our pain—I learned again in El Salvador that the pain of the poor is also the pain of God. I have tried to compare the theology of the poor there with the theology of Europe after Auschwitz, and have again completed the circuit from God as the maker of suffering to God as the sufferer. God suffers with the victims and God transforms their pain. God will deliver them. God will heal the country. The most important image the Bible uses for God's pain in the world is an image from the experience of women, the image of giving birth. In the context of the prophecy of the servant of God in Deutero-Isaiah, is written:

> For a long time I have kept my peace. I have kept still and restrained myself; now I will cry out like a woman in travail. . . . And I will lead the blind in a way that they know not, in paths that they have not known I will guide them. I will turn the darkness before them into light and the rough places into level ground. These are the things I will do and I will not forsake them. [Isaiah 42:14, 16]

In John 16 is written:

> You will be sorrowful, but your sorrow will turn into joy. When a woman is in travail, she has sorrow, because her hour has come; but when she is delivered of the child, she no longer remembers the anguish, for joy that a child is born into the world. So you have sorrow now, but I will see you again and your hearts will rejoice and no one will take your joy from you. [John 16:20b-22]

How does the transformation from fruitless and senseless pain into godly pain take place? How do people get from pain in the kidneys to the pain of labor, which precedes a birth? How is our pain connected with God's pain? And how does God's pain light up in our pain?

Once late one evening I walked along a side street in Manhattan. A beggar squatted on a bundle of rags and I was afraid of this old black man. When I gave him something, he raised his head, looked at me, and said in a clear voice and with great dignity "God bless you." I was moved, but I didn't quite know why. Today I can say that God's pain was visible in his pain. While I was there, my pain changed, my anxiety left me. My anger returned. Everything that Paul writes to the Corinthians about the grief that comes from God came back to me. I was indignant and alarmed at this commonplace street scene. "You offered resistance, you desired change, you called the guilty to account" (2 Cor. 7:11). I knew again why I wish to convert to peace the people I meet, why I can no longer bear the hate and the terror of intimidation of those who tremble at the image of the enemy. The old man who has no roof in the richest country in the history of the world preaches to me, he brings out my pain for his country, which I love and respect. But I have grief also for my own country, which has betrayed its soul in its greed for more arms, in the neurotic passion for greater security. Revulsion against the world in which I live, against its brutality and its avidity for more death, engulfs me. In the middle of this world, where canvasing for the beauty of fighter bombers and tanks is becoming increasingly more elegant and more open, in the middle of this world, under one industry, the profits of the murder industry, the uncontrolled economic growth, where nothing has been learned from Chernobyl, in the middle of this glittering and perfect lie, I am no longer alone with my grief: God's pain embraces my pain. The grief in which we live today becomes a uniting, warring, steadfast strength. My strength grows from my grief.

My entire effort is directed toward the transformation of "worldly grief." I do not believe that it is possible to turn "worldly grief" into rejoicing. That would be to ask too much, as if we could reorganize the deep abyss of grief. It would also be to demand too little, because "worldly grief" would then only be resolved through the joys of the world, which are essentially the joys of having, owning, using, and consuming, or the grief would simply be forgotten and suppressed, rather like a triumphant Christianity drunk from the myth of the resurrection.

When I try to seek help from Paul for a theology after Auschwitz, I must ask whether the expressions "worldly grief" and "godly grief" are indeed applicable to those who have to live after the occurrence of the Holocaust. Under the grief more appropriate to the world, I would then understand a sociological, psychological, and historical interpretation appropriate to scholarship, which not only dispenses with prosecution and defense of God, but also with proximity or distance from God. The renunciation of the metaphysical element leads to an empirical leveling process, to the ability to compare the Holocaust with other crimes, to the statistic of six million people. A grief more appropriate to God would have to appear differently. It would have to perceive God's pain rather than despair in God's omnipotence. It would have to acknowledge God's powerlessness, as Hans Jonas did when he represented—in mythical form—God's renunciation of physical power, of the "strong hand and extended arm," which God used to rescue the people from Egypt.[10]

God's "self-limitation, which makes space for the existence and autonomy of a world," in which evil rises up from human hearts, is the precondition for such a theology stripped of the notions of the patriarchs.

It is our task, I think, to transform "worldly grief" into the pain of God. With the pain of God, I, who live after the Jewish Holocaust and who in recent years have used my strength in the framework of the peace movement against the atomic holocaust, am undergoing a singular experience. The pain is not soothed, calmed, or falsified; it brings me nevertheless a deep joy.

It is as if my hands were touching the power of life, which is also in pain, the pain that indeed, biologically, is life's protest against illness and

death, and which indeed hurts us for the sake of life. I am not talking of
God as an automatic machine that sends peace after pain, and rain after
sun. I see the sun in the rain. I do not wish to seek the power without the
pain, for that would mean separating myself from God and betraying God's
pain. "The people who walked in darkness have seen a great light; those
who dwelt in a land of deep darkness, on them has light shown" (Isaiah
9:1). Whence comes such a precept, if not from the pain of God! How can
we see darkness and light together if not in God, who comprises both!

What I am trying to say sounds mystical, but you know it already and
have often heard it before: it is hidden to Johannes Brahms's piano con-
certo in D minor, because great music deals with God's pain and plunges
into us.

One could object: "I have heard the music of which you speak, but why
should I connect the pain that it expresses with that which you call God?
I have no use for this concept." To this friend I might say: "If the pain
were only pain, I could not term it the pain of God. But because it is
directed toward joy, because it is borne by joy, I can then call it the 'pain
of God.' " This meeting of opposites, joy and pain, this *coincidencia oppos-
itorum* is only very difficult to express in our language because for this
purpose the logic we use is different from that normally used. To experience
such pain is actually close to the overpowering inner experience of birth.
To "bring a child into the world," to give birth, is a primitive experience
in which we come very close to the secret of life. It is an experience that
we undergo and bring about, in which we participate both actively and
passively. It is an experience that challenges the body, spirit, and soul, and
can cause deep changes. It is one of the great experiences of creation in
which we participate. It is a mystical experience, because in this regard we
stand before the secret of life itself. Religions call this secret of life "God"
and my religious tradition includes pain in the secret of life. It places pain
in the heart of God. Jesus calls us to the "participation in the powerlessness
of God in the world" — that is the legacy of the theologian and martyr
Dietrich Bonhoeffer.[11]

If we wish to come to the grief wished by God through worldly grief,
then we must learn to perceive God's pain. Our question will then be: How
should I behave toward the suffering without name of which I am the cause?
How do I stand in relation to the businesses effected by my bank in connection with tortures and racists? How do I deal with the large-scale
destruction of foodstuffs? How am I involved in the war industry (bluntly
termed the "murder industry" by Bertha von Suttner)? How much energy
do I consume and at what cost? How long can I continue to stand being
an accomplice to an unjust system? All these questions belong to the question of suffering. We cannot afford to place this question in a political
pigeonhole and our personal question of suffering in a separate pigeonhole,
as if we only have dealings with God in the confines of our own private
pigeonhole. If we think like that, then we deny God the possibility of draw-

ing our pain into God's pain, we render ourselves incapable of participating in God's pain and experiencing it as the pains of labor.

We do not wish to solve the grief of this world and our pain with the methods of this world, with sedatives. God calls us right in the middle of our pain into kingdom. God wishes to unite our personal history in the great good history of God. How can this be? Hans Jonas says that God has renounced invulnerability. I understand this to mean that God has become vulnerable and only thus is still God, that God has left asceticism behind, and lives as a relationship, a proximity, a dependency on us. "In the beginning was the relationship," says Martin Buber. A theology that takes the pain of God seriously should give something to God, to this suffering, growing, caring God, who should not have to regret having created the world. In Jewish tradition it is the thirty-six just men who support the continuation of the world. That they are just means that they imitate God and—as God does—do what is just: feed the hungry, as God fed Elijah, clothe the naked, as God clothed Adam and Eve, visit those in prison, heal the sick, and bury the dead, as God buried Moses.

I understand the Christian religion as the attempt, which has failed and been betrayed a thousand times, and which still cannot be abandoned, the attempt of heathens to remain true to the God of Israel, who was also the God of Jesus. As I see it, the great danger of Christianity is in its open or latent anti-Judaism, which distances itself triumphantly from the pain of God and comes down on the side of the victor. This essentially or manifestly anti-Jewish manner of thinking appears everywhere where Christianity makes definitions of itself that are not legitimate—not in accord with God's social, political, and historical will. The sects of the new religious claims are an example of this deep anti-Judaism, which manifests itself as wholesome individualism and worship of power: militarism. A Christianity that excludes the Jewish interest, destroys itself: it excludes justice from redemption, politics from theology, this world from the presumed other world, recollection of deliverance from individual suffering and death, and any meaning from nonthematized collective suffering.

If we insist on just action and know that God "has showed you, O man, what is good; and what does the Lord require of you but to do justice, and to love kindness, and to walk humbly with your God?" (Micah 6:8), then we can no longer separate theology and ethics. The Holocaust of the Jews calls us to resist the nuclear holocaust made possible by the excessive accumulation of arms, and waging war against today's and tomorrow's mass murder of the children of debtor nations. Then we will understand God in privation, growth, and suffering in the process of a deliverance, which surpasses our wishes and fears, and calls us to participate in God's being. God seeks what we will become. Where were you, Adam, where are you, Eve, if not in the activity of God that allows us to share God's pain and lives in the heart of God?

NOTES

1. Elie Wiesel, *Der Prozess von Schamgorod* (Paris, 1979; Freiburg, 1987), p. 75.

2. Ibid., p. 115.

3. Ibid.

4. C.-F. Geyer, *Leid und Boeses in philosophischen Deutungen* (Munich, 1983), p. 196.

5. Ibid., p. 107.

6. Ibid., p. 172.

7. Ibid., p. 194.

8. W.R. Jones, *Is God a White Racist?* (New York, 1973).

9. Harold Kushner, *When Bad Things Happen to Good People* (New York, 1982).

10. H. Jonas, *Der Gottesbegriff nach Auschwitz* (Frankfurt, 1987), p. 42.

11. Dietrich Bonhoeffer, *Wilderstand der Ergebung* (Munich, 1954), p. 242 (Letter of July 16, 1944).

10

Economics and Liberation

Can the Theology of Liberation Decide Economic Questions?

NORMAN SOLOMON

THEOLOGY AND ECONOMICS – HOW DO THEY INTERRELATE?

A Shared Problem for Jews and Christians

The nature of the subject of this article means that my disagreements with liberation theologians will be highlighted. This is unfortunate, because it obscures not only the respect I have for many of them as individuals but also the large areas of wholehearted agreement with their aims and attitudes.

The disagreements I shall express are of three kinds: doctrinal, economic, and theological. The first kind will be readily understood; I write as a Jew, and ipso facto reject trinitarian theology and any kind of christology that arises from it. So far as disagreements on economic principles are concerned, I hope that readers will realize that the economic viewpoint I espouse is not specifically Jewish. A large number of Christians would share my views, and indeed the whole point of the article is to demonstrate that these views are not dependent on theology.

What has fascinated me most in writing the article is the third category of disagreement, in the nontrinitarian aspects of theology. Often, where I have ventured to criticize some liberationist view, I have found myself agreeing with mainstream Catholic thought. I am therefore emboldened to ask the reader to accept my words not as a Jewish critique of a Christian philosophy, but as a humble personal contribution to what transpires to be a common Jewish and Christian debate about matters of shared concern.

Nature of the Inquiry

My purpose is to inquire just how far it is proper for a theologian—Jewish or Christian—to go in the critique of society. What are the limits to theological involvement in questions affecting the conduct of society?

I am not questioning the right, even the duty, of theologians to comment on social matters. I am in no way questioning the "prophetic ministry" of synagogue or church. I am simply asking how far it extends.

A trivial example will make the nature of the inquiry clear. The story is told of a certain rather autocratic Lithuanian rabbi in the early part of this century. In the course of his wide learning, he had come across a detailed account by a medieval sage of the process of bricklaying. On the basis of the sage's holiness and authority, he instructed the builders of the town to erect a building along the principles he had "discovered." He refused to heed the protests of expert bricklayers. Of course, the building collapsed. Now, the building was undoubtedly for the public benefit—it is probable that it was some sort of school house. One must therefore concede that the rabbi was right to be concerned that it be erected. It was well within his "prophetic role" to call for schools to be built. It was perhaps within his prophetic role, and certainly within his rabbinic role, to ensure that the school was built in the manner that would best accommodate its educational purposes, and that it be funded in accordance with Jewish principles of justice and fairness, and used for the benefit of poor and rich alike. There are those—evidently he was one of them—who reason that because "the Torah contains everything," it contains the rules for laying bricks. I believe this to be a wrong view of holy scripture; but even if it were correct, its advocates would still have to demonstrate, which they cannot, just how the rules for bricklaying, or carpentry, or computer programming, or whatever else, are to be derived from the Torah, the Qur'an, the thoughts of Mao, or whatever they happen to regard as a holy text. Because no one has done this with the slightest cogency, it can confidently be asserted that there are limits to theological involvement in social questions, if only at the level of technical implementation.

The hard question to decide—and it is the one to which I address myself—is just where "matters of social concern" end and technical problems take over. It is almost certainly not possible to draw a sharp line between the two, but it is still clear that some matters are on one side of the fuzzy line and some on the other, and that along the fuzzy line itself one has to exercise special caution.

To narrow the discussion to manageable size, only those aspects of the theology of liberation will be considered which relate to economic matters; the conclusions would have force also with regard to political matters, or in any area where a specialized body of nontheological knowledge and expertise exists. Politics and economics are only to a limited extent technologies like bricklaying, but it would be a serious error to disregard this aspect of these disciplines.

Economics and politics cannot neatly be separated. However, I am quite deliberately concentrating on economics rather than politics, because it seems to me that liberation theologians too easily slip into the error of assuming that if power (political) structures are changed, the economic problems—the creation and distribution of wealth—will somehow solve themselves.

Questions To Be Asked

As well as being on our guard against the slipshod assumption that some unspecified change of power structure will magically assure the generation and just distribution of wealth, we must constantly bear in mind the following questions:

(a) What are the ultimate economic aims formulated for society by theologians of liberation?

(b) Granted that liberation theologians are justified in their complaints about economic exploitation in Latin America and elsewhere, does it follow that "the (economic) system" as such is not the best available? Does the fault lie in the people who operate it, rather than in the system itself?

(c) If "the system" is not the best available, what alternative is proposed in its place?

(d) Can theology decide between the competing claims of different economic systems to achieve the ultimate aims the theologians have formulated?

Does Liberation Theology Require a Distinctive Economics?

Is it perhaps missing the whole point of liberation theology even to ask such questions? A superficial glance at the writings of liberation theologians—most of whom would in any case maintain that their praxis rather than their theorizing is what matters—reveals such headings as "liberation and salvation," "eschatology and politics," "the scandal of poverty," "liberation praxis and Christian faith," and the like, none of which headings would figure in a standard text book of economics.

On the other hand, a closer inspection will undoubtedly yield statements with serious economic import. There will be talk of a "preferential option for the poor," and in many cases there will be a liberal sprinkling of Marxist jargon, even if the writer with justification denies that he is himself a Marxist. Indeed, there is no way one can express solidarity with the poor—and "poor" in the context of liberation theology includes, if it is not exhausted by, those lacking material goods—without involving economic consequences. If one complains about the maldistribution of wealth, one ipso facto calls for its more just distribution. If one views the maldistribution as a consequence of "the system" rather than of the failings and greed of individuals, one is in effect calling for either a modification or a replacement of the system. It is undeniably the prophetic role of religion, and well within the ancient traditions of Judaism and Christianity, not to mention others, to criticize society, even in a radical way. If, as Gustavo Gutiérrez claims,[1] Latin America is a "subcontinent of oppression and pillage," there is no doubt that religious people, together with all others who care, should shout aloud and spare no efforts to achieve change. Everyone should admire the courage and the moral fire of those Latin American men and women of the spirit who have given up their comfortable lives in city and religious community to go out into the wilderness wastelands to identify with the poor and the oppressed. The basic communities they have created are a symbol of light and hope for our times.

But the question addressed by this essay is not whether the basic communities are symbols of hope and light for our times, but whether they, or the theology of liberation in general, constitute the most effective response to the maldistribution of wealth, or to the other major issues they seek to highlight. It may well be that theologians, or prophets, are not the right people to solve such problems, even if they are an appropriate group to demand a solution. But if they cannot, qua theologians or prophets, solve the problems, they should be careful not to give the impression that they are solving them, or by loose talk to lead people to think that they have committed themselves to particular economic or political viewpoints.

Compassion or Effective Help?

I will return later to a consideration of the "preferential option for the poor." Here I must pose, but not attempt to answer, the radical question of whether an option for the poor is the answer to the problem of injustice. Gregory Baum[2] has defined the preferential option for the poor as "the double commitment, implicit in Christian discipleship, to look upon the social reality from the perspective of the marginalized and to give public witness of one's solidarity with their struggle for justice." While not questioning the second of these commitments, or the compassion of the first, I am asking whether the first provides the right vantage point for effectively combating injustice. If my neighbor has a leaky tap, my sharing his suffering of the effects of leaky taps will not get the tap mended. Sufficient (but not excessive) compassion is necessary to see that something is amiss; my next task is not to *share* the leaking tap, but to send for an expert plumber. Why should economic problems require a different approach?

LINKS WITH JUDAISM — BIBLE, PRAXIS

Since the earliest days of the theology of liberation it has been clear that there is much in its way of talking that is resonant with Jewish themes and concerns. Already in January 1975 the World Council of Churches and the International Jewish Committee on Interreligious Affairs—neither of them Catholic nor predominantly South American organizations—met in London, England, for a dialogue of Jews and Christians on the concept of power, at which many of the themes of the theology of liberation were aired.[3] In 1984 Dan Cohn-Sherbok, listing ways in which the gap between Jews and Christians may be narrowing today, referred to "another cause for hope which has as yet remained unexplored." The unexplored avenue (as we have just seen, it was not entirely unexplored) turned out to be liberation theology for, says Cohn-Sherbok, "it is obvious that liberation theologians have relied heavily on the central biblical themes of freedom from oppression, justice, and the role of the saving remnant. . . . They have revitalized and readapted the teachings of the Old Testament . . . in the modern world where the rich and the poor live side by side. In the light of this return to Jewish sources, it is now possible for both faiths to work together in trust and hope."[4]

Certainly, the extensive use of Tanakh ("Old Testament") and concern for the "real," historical Jesus, found in the writings of Leonardo Boff and other liberation theologians, will echo in many Jewish hearts. As against that, there is the danger (recognized by Boff) that Christian typological exegesis will cancel the "bond" established with Judaism through the Hebrew scriptures. It is too easy for Christians to read the "Old Testament" as having no significance other than as preparing the way for the "New." Fortunately, nowadays most serious theologians have learned to avoid the pitfall into which popular writers still stumble of reading from Genesis to Exodus chapter 12 and then skipping to Matthew as if nothing—not Torah at Sinai, and not the land—came between.

As well as the scriptural link with Judaism, many have alleged a parallel in the emphasis on praxis, which appears at first sight to be akin to our traditional Jewish emphasis on *halaka* (law, practice) rather than theology—as one of our first-century sages, Simon the son of Gamaliel, put it, *lo hamidrash ha-iqar ela ha-maase*, which I may translate freely, "what matters most is practice, not theory." However, any such link should be interpreted with caution. "Traditional Jewish emphasis on *halaka* (law, practice) rather than theology" presupposes that the system of *halaka* itself be taken seriously; what it devalues is theology. Simon was not making the point that theology ought to take second place to *halaka*, but simply that the study of *halaka* ought not to be pursued to the detriment of its practice. Liberation theologians are not calling for a system of *halaka*, nor are they devaluing theology per se; they are urging people to "get out into the field" and share in the sufferings of the poor. The most that can be safely claimed is that liberation theologians share with Jews an emphasis on the concrete expression of faith. But I suspect that many Christian theologians would share this emphasis without identifying with the liberationist trend.

Another link with Judaism is the new attitude to poverty. Christians in the past have tended to make a virtue of poverty, but Gutiérrez and others have claimed that the poverty idealized by Christians is not the dehumanizing lack of material goods, but the humility of spirit and the commitment to solidarity with the poor.

Biblical Models

Liberation theologians have made much use of the Exodus and prophetic paradigms of the Hebrew scriptures. Let us see what these paradigms are and what might be their relevance to critiques of the "socio-economic system."

The Exodus Paradigm — There have been some very sophisticated analyses of exodus theology. Leaving aside typological interpretations (these are found mutais mutandis among Jewish as well as Christian exegetes), it would be fascinating to compare, for instance, John Pawlikowski's four-stage model of liberation (faith in God's saving acts in history, communitarian spirituality, link between liberation and Torah, and Mitzvot, movement from political to inner freedom) with Leon Klenicki's model, based on S. R. Hirsch's philosophy, of "overcoming inner and outer bondage" (experience of God's redeeming presence, freedom to become a covenantal community in one's own land, the service of God through Torah and Mitzvot); all the same elements appear to be present.

Our task is, fortunately, a simpler one. What are the bare essentials that emerge from a plain reading of the Exodus text? How far does the account in Exodus of the bondage of the Hebrew slaves in Egypt correspond with the state of the desperately poor in Brazil?

The Hebrew slaves in Egypt were an oppressed class. They were in some sense "conscientized" by Moses, they were freed from bondage, they were brought to Sinai and given a "message" there by God.

All this suggests some parallels with the South American situation, but there are significant differences.

The Israelites in Egypt were a minority, unlike the masses of the poor in Latin America. They were foreigners, which on the one hand was an alienating factor contributing to the sense of homelessness and deprivation, but on the other hand meant that, unlike the South American poor, they did not have the experience of being persecuted primarily by their own brethren. The "conscientization" they received through Moses was nothing to do with "the causes of poverty," but a reminder of their identity as children of Abraham, Isaac, and Jacob, with whom God had been bound by the promise of a land of their own. The "freedom" promised and given was a freedom from subjection to the taskmasters of Egypt. The "message" at Sinai was a detailed constitution for their society; it is significant that the "new order for society" — the Torah — was proclaimed by God, and did *not* arise from the "basic community" of Israelites. Indeed, the Israelites themselves seem to have done very little at any stage to bring about their own redemption; God—not even Moses—is the prime actor on the stage, to such an extent that Jews find it at most curious, not disturbing, that the very name of Moses is omitted from the account of the Exodus read at Passover.

The Exodus text of the story of the Egyptian bondage does not offer an explicit paradigm for a critique on "the causes of poverty." Exodus does not seem concerned with explaining causes, other than historical ones, for oppression. And when Ezekiel (16:4-7) takes up the theme, he offers no critique of the Egyptian economic system, only a condemnation of Israel's sins. Theologians of liberation do not engage in scathing denunciation of the sins of the South American poor, pointing to it as the cause of their oppression, and quite rightly so; though surely the ancient Israelites were not more or less sinful than the present-day South American poor.

It is true that the Israelites were not "conscientized" to their situation before Moses and Aaron came, and only with rising awareness of their situation did they "cry out unto the Lord." But, as we have said, the "conscientization" they received through Moses had to do not with "the causes of poverty," but with their identity as children of Abraham, Isaac, and Jacob to whom God had made the promise. It is legitimate for us to argue that the Egyptian "system," if that can be blamed for pharaoh's works of self-aggrandizement and the accompanying forced labor, was a "cause" of Hebrew bondage. The Bible itself, however, does not assign it as the cause.

Is there, then, nothing in the Exodus story that would indicate a concern with "the system"? Quite the contrary. The Torah, whether specifically at Sinai or in the numerous sections of legislation in the Hebrew Bible, is at great pains to delineate a "system" in which injustices shall not prevail; the constant concern of the prophets is that it shall be implemented. But the system does not *arise from* the people, it is *addressed to* the people by God, as the terms of covenant with them.

That "the system" of Torah is concerned with macro as well as micro economics there is no shadow of doubt. The sabbatical year, the cancellation of debts, the return of slaves in the Jubilee, are all measures clearly designed to prevent or ameliorate the exploitation of small-holders that individuals by wealthy landowners, and indeed to prevent the growth of a class of wealthy landowners. Typically, they are specific legislative acts rather than generalized prophetic calls.

Prophetic Models—All prophets have in common is that sin is the cause of evil and suffering, and that the root sin is idolatry, which is essentially "unfaithfulness" to God. Beyond that, there are three levels in the prophetic response to poverty:

1) Elijah represents the "band-aid" level of concern. He acts on a specific problem, be it the nationally significant "case" of Naboth's vineyard, or the private "case" of the poor widow of Zarephath in Sidon. Elijah is the master of the ad hoc miracle.

2) Amos performs no miracles. Instead, he ruthlessly exposes the heart of social injustice:

> Because they sell the innocent for silver
> and the destitute for a pair of shoes;
> they grind the heads of the poor into the earth
> and thrust the humble out of their way.
>
> [Amos 2:6, 7]

Amos wants to change people, rather than "the system":

> Seek good and not evil
> that you may live . . .
> Hate evil and love good;
> enthrone justice in the courts. [Amos 5:14, 15]

3) Moses alone is concerned with what we might call "the system." He is sent to free the slaves and provide them with a land and with a constitution, the Torah. The Torah is "the system."

THE OPTION FOR THE POOR

What Is the "Preferential Option"?

Gregory Baum[5] has defined the preferential option for the poor as "the double commitment, implicit in Christian discipleship, to look upon the social reality from the perspective of the marginalized and to give public witness of one's solidarity with their struggle for justice."

The editors of a collection of papers state: "The preferential option for solidarity with the poor is nothing short of a Copernican revolution for the Church. The protagonist in history and society who henceforth implements the Christian mission will be the poor . . . who are the privileged bearers of the message."[6]

I cannot pass judgment on whether the preferential option is a Copernican revolution in Christianity, though one wonders whether such Christians as Francis of Assisi were not at least precursors. So far as Judaism is concerned, however, the "preferential option" is not startling. The Talmud states, for instance: "Take care with the children of the poor — it is from them that Torah shall come forth to Israel. If any poor person shall claim (in extenuation on the Day of) Judgment 'I was poor and distracted by the need to obtain food' they [the heavenly judges] will reply to him: 'You were certainly no poorer than Hillel.' "[7]

It is worth recalling, in these days when the affluence of North American Jewry forms the popular image of what Jews are, that the historical reality

of Jewish communities has been of intense poverty. Even today the affluence of the few should not obscure the deprivation of the many.

The Need for Balanced Perspectives

One must, however, place the "preferential option" in a balanced context, and this is where not only I, as a Jew, but apparently the mainstream
Catholic Church, have reservations, at least with regard to some of the
more extreme expressions of "preference." Is Baum suggesting, when he
instructs Christians "to look upon the social reality from the perspective of
the marginalized," that one should look upon the social reality *exclusively*
from the perspective of the marginalized? God, and even we humans, are
not so simpleminded that we are limited to one perspective. Indeed, situations are rarely so simple that one individual is in all respects "the marginalized" and another "the oppressor." In the context of the Middle East,
for instance, it is easy to see that Israel, with respect to the neighboring
states that wish to undermine it or destroy it, is "marginalized." This is
perfectly consistent with the Israelite perception of Palestinians as "marginalized." Or to take a still broader example, women, in virtually all known
societies, are "marginalized" by men; children and animals are "marginalized" by all humans, including women. To state, as an absolute, that one
should "look upon the social reality from the perspective of the marginalized" is to ignore the limited nature of all perspectives other than the
divine, which is infinite.

When we are told (Deuteronomy 10:19) "You shall love the stranger,
for you were strangers in Egypt," we are taught to *appreciate* the perspective
of the stranger, the "marginalized;" but we are not taught that this is the
exclusive perspective from which to view the world.

Once anything becomes exclusive, it is an idol. We must reject idolatry
of the poor as surely as we reject the idolatry of riches or power.

Does God show favor to the poor? Surely God shows favor to those who
love God and obey God's commandments, irrespective of whether they are
rich or poor. God's "principle," if so we may put it, is to help those in need,
those who suffer oppression; this is the theme of many of God's commandments.

God's Torah is universal, and does not favor one social stratum over
another. Unlike the codes of the "nations round about," it does not have
one law for the freeman, one for the slaves; all are equal in God's eyes,
the rich and the poor among them. That is why scripture repeatedly insists,
in its legislative sections, on attention to the marginalized elements within
society—women, orphans, Levites, strangers—that the preferential *attention* given them might lead to equal treatment.

Hence: "You shall not pervert justice, either by favoring the poor or by
subservience to the great" (Leviticus 19:5).

Identification exclusively with the poor leads to confrontation, hatred, and strife, "either-or" attitudes, divisions, one-sidedness.

Identification exclusively with the poor leads to absorbing the prejudices of the poor, such as that the wealthy are wicked, or that "those in power" — the USA, the multinationals, the employers, the government—are wicked. Some of them are wicked, no doubt. But so are some of the poor.

In his 1981 encyclical *Laborem Exercens* the pope argues strongly for solidarity of workers:

> Therefore, one must continue to investigate the "subject" of labor and the conditions in which one lives. To create social justice in different parts of the world, in different countries and their interrelationships, there is always a need for *new movements of solidarity with* working people *and for solidarity with* working people. Such solidarity must always be present where the social degradation of the subject of work, the exploitation of the workers, and the increasing burdens of misery, even famine, require it. The church is strongly pledged to this cause, for she considers it her mission, her service, as she confirms her faith in Christ, where truly she is to be "the church of the poor." And "the poor" appear in many guises . . . often as a *consequence of the violation of the dignity of human labor* . . . the plague of unemployment . . . the devaluation of . . . the right to a just wage, to personal security.[8]

A proper balance ought to have led to his calling unequivocally for solidarity of workers and management. In the later *Sollicitudo Rei Socialis* he seems more clearly to recognize the inherent divisiveness of calls to workers' exclusive solidarity when he draws attention to the broader groupings of society: "By virtue of her own evangelical duty, the church feels called to take her stand beside the poor, to discern the justice of their requests, and to help satisfy them, without losing sight of the good of groups in the context of the common good."[9] In this last phrase, "without losing sight . . . ," John Paul II wisely, if not with great emphasis, acknowledges the need for a plurality of perspectives in addressing the problems of society.

Theology and Social Perspectives

The concern of liberation theologians with the "historical Jesus" attracts a warm response from Jews, for this is a level upon which they feel they can "handle" the Jesus story.

However, as is natural for Christian theologians but anathema to Jews, this historical, suffering Jesus is seen as the incarnation of God. A new christology ensues, that of the suffering God identified with the poor. This becomes the rationale for Baum's call to the "double commitment, implicit in Christian discipleship, to look upon the social reality from the perspective of the marginalized and to give public witness of one's solidarity with their struggle for justice."

The argument is of course backwards, as everyone knows that liberation theologians have based their christology on their social theories rather than vice versa. The ideology has become an epiphenomenon of the social struggle, to use Marxist terms; perhaps this is what is meant when we are told that theology is a "reflection on praxis." If they had started with christology, they could scarcely have failed to notice that Catholic Christianity has a Christ in majesty as well as a suffering servant. As strongly as I, a Jew, reject all forms of incarnational christology, it seems clear enough that if one is to express one's understanding of God in incarnational terms at all, there must either be multiple incarnations, as in Indian religions, or a multifaceted incarnation, as provided by the varied images of Christ that figure in traditional Christian thought. The suffering servant figure—the "marginalized" historical Jesus—can be part of the imagery, but does not of itself express the wholeness of God.

In the Hebrew scriptures there is no such problem, as the incarnation-free imagery of God is protean in expression, ranging from the "mighty warrior" to the "compassionate father" to the shepherd who accompanies those who walk through the valley of the shadow of death (Psalm 23). There is a wholeness in the vision of God that precludes identification with a particular section of society. Certainly, God is with the poor. But was God not also with David and the kings so long as they walked in God's ways?

Few rabbinic passages more convincingly demonstrate the biblical balance in the concept of God and hence of society than the following:

> Rabbi Yochanan said, in every passage where thou findest the greatness of God mentioned, there thou findest also his humility. This is written in the Torah, repeated in the Prophets, and a third time started in the Writings. It is written in the Torah, For the Lord your God, he is God of gods, and Lord of lords, the great, mighty, and revered God, who showeth no partiality, nor taketh a bribe. And it is written afterwards, He doth execute justice for the fatherless and widow, and loveth the stranger, in giving him food and raiment. It is repeated in the Prophets, as it is written, For thus saith the high and lofty One that inhabiteth eternity, and whose name is Holy, I dwell in the high and holy place, with him also that is of a contrite and humble spirit, to revive the spirit of the humble, and to revive the heart of the contrite ones. It is a third time stated in the Writings, Sing unto God, sing praises unto his Name: extol ye him that rideth upon the heavens whose name is the Lord, and rejoice before him. And it is written afterwards, A father of the fatherless, and a judge of the widows, is God in his holy habitation.[10]

SOCIALISM/MARXISM

"Structures of Sin"—To Change or Not To Change "the System"

Liberation theologians are divided between those who unequivocally wish to "change the system" and those who favor working with the basic communities rather than tackling "the system" head on.

"The system" has to be changed because it is "a structure of sin." The pope accepts the liberationist terminology of "structures of sin," but is it a helpful concept? A "structure of sin" is not a particular type of socio-economic system, defined in socio-economic terms, but a socio-economic system in which people are motivated by greed, lust, and sinful stimuli generally. This is a very confused way to categorize socio-economic systems. People living under any known socio-economic system may individually and in specific instances act through altruistic or through selfish motives; but these are characteristics of people, not of socio-economic systems.

What seems to underlie the concept is the Marxist idea that the nature of the capitalist system was such that capitalists were bound to exploit labor, hence greed was actually built into the system; in a classless, socialist society this would not happen. The refutation of this simplistic notion may be observed daily in socialist societies; they are no more free from greed, envy, corruption, and other human evils than are capitalist societies.

There may be some difference of opinion between Jews and Augustinian Christians as to whether humankind is *inherently* evil (carries a burden of sin from Adam), but there is no disagreement that humankind has a considerable *propensity* to evil. If one were not convinced of this on theological grounds, one need only turn to Freudian and subsequent depth psychology for confirmation (though "evil" is itself a theological rather than a psychological category).

Of course, some "systems" lend themselves to particular types of evil. A system might depend on slavery (in the literal old-fashioned though not yet obsolete sense rather than the metaphorical "wage-slave" sense of the Marxists). It is interesting that the Bible (and indeed the church, until recently) did not oppose the "system," though it certainly modified it and sought to ameliorate its harshness; the actual abolition of slavery was the achievement of modern Western industrialized society.

The great Portuguese Jewish philosopher Isaac Abarbanel (1437-1508)[11] held that there would be no government in the days of the messiah, for all forms of government lead to domination of one human being by another, and are by nature restrictive and repressive; government is only required at the present time owing to the sinfulness of humankind. He did realize that this would mean a return to a very primitive sort of existence, where people would live directly on the bounty of nature, abandoning all technology and presumably trade. Clearly liberation theologians share with me the rejection of this ideal, and would like those whom they serve to partake in the benefits—health services, good food, clean water, education, and the like—that are now the prerogative of the wealthier nations. There is no way this can be attained without complex economic and hence political structures.

I hold it to be a cornerstone of theology that where there are human relations, there is the opportunity to sin. The more complex that set of relationships—as in world trade at the present time—the more complex are the opportunities to sin.

No one has designed a sin-proof system. Surely, the church itself, viewed as a social structure, is not claimed to be a sinproof supranational structure. Who would deny that its priests and officials are subject to ambition and other vices, just like members of secular structures? The vagueness of liberationists in calling for a "new system" is patent. Some are in danger of slipping into a sort of Marxist utopianism. Even as perceptive a theologian as Leonardo Boff, who argues that liberation theologians seek a *participatory democracy*, not actual socialism as it is in force in any existing country, evades the question by implying that the new economic order can only be formulated by the participatory democracy.[12] It is disappointing that he does not note the danger of calling for a revolution that has no clearly defined program.

There are three principal dangers in calling for radical revision of the system when one cannot say what is to be put in its place and how. First, such a call destabilizes society, thus providing opportunity for the strong-armed and the unscrupulous (of left or of right) to take charge. Second, it distracts people from constructive criticism of the existing system. Third, the absence of a clearly formulated alternative generates confusion and false hopes.

The way ahead lies not in the revolutionary substitution of novel socio-economic systems for the present ones, but in the difficult and painstaking evolutionary process of curbing abuses that arise within the system. Moralists and preachers have a dual role in this process. They must persuade individuals to act in an upright and moral fashion, explaining how traditional values can be upheld in a modern society. They must also urge legislators to enshrine appropriate values in their laws.[13]

I would unhesitatingly align myself with those liberation theologians who concentrate on developing the basic communities rather than calling for radical revision of "the system."

Self-Interest and Social Well-Being

Judaism, like the other great religious traditions, unambiguously condemns the pursuit of wealth for its own sake as a major evil, responsible through envy and greed for human conflict and for turning humankind away from God.

Yet modern industrialized society confronts us with a paradox that was not grasped by the men and women of the past, to whom we turn for spiritual guidance. It was first clearly perceived in the eighteenth century that, subject to certain necessary restraints, the pursuit of self-interest results in the enhancement—Adam Smith claimed the maximization—of social well-being. The idea is central to Smith's economic philosophy, and it is well to remember that this classic advocate of laissez-faire economics also formulated the classic expression of the need for appropriate government controls:

The sovereign has only three duties to attend to. . . . First, the duty of protecting the society from the violence and invasion of independent societies; secondly, the duty of protecting, as far as possible, every member of the society from the injustice or oppression of every other member of it, or the duty of establishing an exact administration of justice; and, thirdly, the duty of erecting and maintaining certain public works and certain institutions, which it can never be for the interest of any individual, or small number of individuals, to erect and maintain, because the profit could never repay the expense to any individual or small number of individuals, though it may frequently do much more than repay it to a great society.[14]

Much of the subsequent economic history of Western countries has been bound up with the manner and extent in which the third of these duties should be implemented.

Karl Marx, of course, attacked Smith's concept that the pursuit of self-interest results in the maximization of social well-being. Marx argued that the "dominant mode of production"—that is, the ownership of the means of production—meant that "inevitably" (one of his favorite but most dangerous terms) workers would be "exploited" (another dangerous key term) by entrepreneurs.

It cannot be part of my brief in this essay to argue for or against Marxist economics; those interested must study the works of such as Van Mises, Lange, Hayek, Pareto, Popper, and the Friedmans, to name but a few. I wish to comment only on the theological implications of the debate, by drawing attention to two questions.

First, is there any way in which the classic debates of economics can be settled on a genuinely theological basis? Curiously, among both Jews and Christians there have been found thinkers who would maintain that socialism is the true expression of their faith, and also thinkers diametrically opposed to this view, to whom only a free enterprise system harmonizes with the values taught by their faith. On the socialist side, we have the liberationist Mexican ex-Jesuit José Porfirio Miranda.[15] Miranda is presumably unacquainted with the writings of the early religious socialist Zionists, but his conviction that socialism is the only just system and is therefore what his religion is all about is matched by theirs. What they also have in common is the lack of a serious critique of socialism or a serious examination of alternative and mixed systems. Their argument seems to be: socialism is the most just possible system for the organization of human society; faith demands social justice; therefore faith demands socialism. In this way, one is bamboozled into thinking that their socialism is based on their theology. In fact it is not, for the truth of the first premise—that socialism is the most just possible system for the organization of human society—is precisely what remains unproven. Moreover, the only relevant ways to demonstrate the truth of this premise are nontheological.

Second, how can traditional theology, Jewish or Christian, with its antipathy to the pursuit of wealth, come to terms with the elements of truth in the view that the pursuit of self-interest results in the enhancement (I do not say maximization) of social well-being? Although the matter is by no means as straightforward as Smith thought, it is a readily observable fact that those nations in which there has been the fullest development of free enterprise have also produced, with the surplus wealth they have generated, the best living conditions for their citizens. Traditional theology would have forecast only disaster from such unchaining of self-interest.

Wealth Creation and Identification with the Poor

Julio de Santa Ana, in an impassioned essay,[16] remarks how, "during the sixties, hardly anyone spoke about the situation of the poor. Poverty seemed simply something that was inevitably about to be eradicated." The rich nations were about to help the developing nations to become rich themselves. The hopes proved illusory. Santa Ana, following Furtado (and, at some distance, Marx), explains that the poor nations remained poor because the rich nations used mercantile means to extract surplus value from them. He seems to think that this is inevitable: "So we have to say that *development and underdevelopment are two faces of the same coin*" (his emphasis).

Santa Ana has every right to be passionate, as he has before him the memory of the exploitation of the native Americans by the Conquistadores—and the reality of present-day poverty. But one must be careful in suggesting comparisons. The Conquistadores quite openly set out to plunder, conquer, take over the lands of the Americas for themselves, and with some honorable exceptions were unconcerned with the welfare and culture of the conquered. But the nations assembled at Bretton Woods in 1944 to set up a new world economic order had already, by and large, rejected exploitive imperialism, even though paternalistic attitudes persisted. The World Bank and the IMF may have failed, as Santa Ana claims, to halt the growth of poverty in Brazil and other countries, but there is no doubt that that has been their consistent aim.

Is it true, as he claims, that "*the international order agreed at Bretton*

Woods is incapable of eradicating poverty from our societies" (his emphasis again)? I happen to disagree strongly with this assertion and believe that the causes of persistent poverty in Brazil and other countries lie else-where—after all, countries such as South Korea have successfully evolved from underdeveloped to developed under the same external conditions. The point I wish to make here is that, whatever the reasons for the failure of the rich nations, despite their honorable intentions, to rescue the undeveloped nations from poverty, these reasons can only be ascertained by careful economic argument and analysis, not by theology.

I therefore feel wronged when I hear that in the name of religion in general, or Christianity in particular, poor and previously uneducated men and women are being "conscientized" into a realization of the "causes of poverty" by being exposed to this type of economic philosophy. They do not yet have the critical apparatus to assess what they hear, and can too easily be led into hatred of and confrontation with the "devil," who is alleged to be the source of all their ills. This is bad in itself, like all causeless hatred; it also diverts them from discovering the real causes of their poverty. The so-called Freire method[17] cheats by pretending to work in a "bottom-up" manner; ideas on power structure are implicit in the very language with which the teachers cajole "spontaneous" responses from their pupils, and from a political point of view at least, there is a clear "top-down" indoctrination.

This matter is not one on which Catholics are divided from Jews; I know that my feelings are shared by a good many Catholics. On the other hand, there are some Jews who agree with Julio de Santa Ana. Marc Ellis, for instance, writes: "Capitalism, as practiced, may represent affluence for the few; it means unemployment and poverty for many." There is at least a hint in this sentence that a better form of capitalism might exist than the one currently practiced, but there is far too ready an acceptance of Marxist jargon. Ellis, like de Santa Ana, has been led by his righteous passion for the cause of the poor into a failure to distinguish a theological problem from a political or economic one.

It is interesting that de Santa Ana argues his whole case on economic grounds—"argues" may not be the right word, for he assumes rather than argues Marxist principles. His detailed and reasoned arguments are *within* rather than *for* his system of thought. Be that as it may, there remains an unbridged gap between liberation theology *as theology* and the economic doctrines espoused by its advocates.

It seems to me that this is just as it should be. For there is in reality *no connection* between theological views on poverty and specific economic analyses of the causes of poverty.

CONCLUSION

As to "the system," I have made clear that I favor evolution, not revolution. Judgments in politics, economics, and other technical subjects must be grounded in the special knowledge of those subjects. Theology may lay down broad aims—help the poor, seek peace, cease exploitation—but these aims must be implemented through the increasing knowledge available to us in the social and natural sciences, not through woolly ideologies and ignorance of the "facts on the ground."

In this, it is unlikely that my views differ at all from those of any Christian of similar temperament and cultural background. We can both share in learning from the deeds of persons "seized by the spirit," as we recognize so many liberationists to be. We can also share in disentangling true insight from false ideology, and specifically in disentangling theology from politics and economics—which is not to deny the former a role in shaping the broad aims of the latter.

We must be on our guard against any form of "utopian heresy." And those of us who think of ourselves as theologians would do well to heed the words of Cardinal Ratzinger who, in a letter criticizing liberation theology, writes "liberation is first and foremost liberation from the radical slavery of sin. . . . As a logical consequence, it calls for freedom from many different kinds of slavery in the cultural, economic, social, and political spheres."[18] I do not share the cardinal's views on sin and atonement, but my Jewish heritage teaches me that ultimately the success of any social or economic system depends not so much on its draftsmanship as on the sinfulness or otherwise of those who operate it.

And in point of fact no one knows how to draft the utopian economic system, as noted above. If the new order cannot yet be described, what basis is there for the critique of present economic practice, other than that it results in deprivation for many? Even this is questionable; without the present economic order, the poor would presumably be deprived anyway, though they might not notice it, for no one would be rich. "All men and women of good will" agree that we ought to help the poor, and that in economic (though not judicial) matters, they should have some form of "preferential option." If theology gets us no further than that, it is superfluous. What we really need to know is how to combine effective wealth creation with just distribution. This demands the specialized knowledge of economists, sociologists, and politicians rather than theologians or newly "conscientized" peasants.

NOTES

1. Gustavo Gutiérrez, *A Theology of Liberation* (Maryknoll, N.Y.: Orbis Books, 1973).

2. Gregory Baum, "Option for the Powerless," *Ecumenist*, 26/1 (Nov./Dec. 1987).

3. A summary of the consultation was published under the joint auspices of the two bodies and appeared as item SE/85 in *Study Encounter*, Vol. 11, no. 4 (Geneva: World Council of Churches, 1975).

4. Dan Cohn-Sherbok, "Jews, Christians and Liberation Theology," in *Christian Jewish Relations*, vol. 17 (London, March 1984). A fuller development of his ideas may be found in his book, *On Earth as It Is in Heaven: Jews, Christians, and Liberation Theology*, published by Orbis Books, Maryknoll, N.Y. 1987. See also *Toward a Jewish Theology of Liberation*, by Marc H. Ellis, Orbis Books, Maryknoll, N.Y., 1987.

5. Baum, "Option."

6. *Concilium: Option for the Poor: Challenge to the Rich Countries*, L. Boff and V. Elizondo, eds. (Edinburgh: Clark, 1986), p. ix.

7. Babylonian Talmud, *Yoma* 35b. Hillel was one of the great teachers at the beginning of the first century; he was a poor Babylonian immigrant.

8. John Paul II, *Laborem Exercens*, especially #8.

9. John Paul II, *Sollicitudo Rei Socialis*, #39.

10. Yochanan bar Nappacha, who died in 279, was a leading Palestinian rabbi. This discourse is found in the Babylonian Talmud, *Megilla* 31a; the translation is that of the slightly different version in the prayers for the conclusion of the Sabbath, as they appear in the *Authorized Daily Prayer Book*, edited by J. H. Hertz (London, 1941).

11. See in particular his commentary on Genesis 2. For a summary in English of Abarbanel's messianic teaching, see B. Netanyahu, *Abravanel* (Philadelphia, 1953), pp. 195-257.

12. See his article in "Jews, Christians, and Liberation Theology," a symposium published as the spring 1988 issue of the journal *Christian Jewish Relations* (London: Institute of Jewish Affairs).

13. See the long citation from Adam Smith in the section below. Smith was very much aware of the need for legislative support for the implementation of values in society.

14. Adam Smith, *An Inquiry into the Nature and Causes of the Wealth of Nations* (1776), Book 4, Chapter 9.

15. J. P. Miranda, *Marx and the Bible: A Critique of the Philosophy of Oppression* (Maryknoll, N.Y.: Orbis Books, 1974).

16. Julio de Santa Ana, "How Rich Nations Came To Be Rich" in *Concilium: Option for the Poor: Challenge to the Rich Countries*.

17. See P. Freire, *Education for Critical Consciousness* (New York: Seabury Press, 1973), and *Pedagogy of the Oppressed* (New York: Herder & Herder, 1970).

18. *Instruction on Certain Aspects of the Theology of Liberation*, August 1984.

POSTSCRIPT

Jews, Christians, and Liberation Theology

A Response

MARC H. ELLIS

The ecumenical dialogue between Jews and Christians, at least as we have known it since the Second Vatican council, is over. Or to put it more succinctly, the dialogue has reached an impasse that can be surmounted only with an honesty that heretofore has been absent. With this honesty comes an unexpected reversal: if Jewish participants in the ecumenical dialogue have generally set the agenda for almost three decades, today it is imperative for Christians to take the lead. This is because the essential framework of dialogue has shifted from an accounting for Christian complicity in the suffering of Jews, most recently in the Holocaust, to a Jewish need for repentance in the oppression of the Palestinian people.

Let me explain. From the beginning, the emphasis in dialogue between Christians and Jews has been on historic Christian anti-Jewishness and the saga of Jews as an innocent, suffering people. Thus Christians have been asked to look at their history through the travail of the Jews, with the concomitant reinterpretation of anti-Judaic elements within, for example, the New Testament, church teachings, and ritual expressions of faith. In short, Christians are asked to cleanse their tradition of anti-Judaic elements and to set a course that recognizes and affirms both their biblical patrimony and contemporary Jewish history as authentic in and of itself. But ecumenical dialogue has also been raised in the context of what might be termed the "ecumenical deal" — that is, the recognition that biblical patrimony and contemporary Jewish history lead to an embrace of a particular theme of post-Holocaust Jewish life, commitment to the state of Israel. From the

Jewish side, the embrace of Israel as central to Jewish survival and continuation as a people is suggested—often demanded—and is linked with the
authenticity of Christian repentance for past sins against the Jewish people.

Therefore—within the context of the ecumenical deal—any retreat on
the Christian side in support of Israel is ipso facto a retreat from Christian
repentance in relation to Jewish suffering. Within this framework, from the
Jewish side, it makes perfect sense to equate criticism of Israel with anti-
Jewishness. From the Christian side it makes perfect sense to question
whether a Christian critique of Israel is in fact anti-Jewish. Thus the ecumenical deal is characterized by a demand on the Jewish side and silence
on the Christian side, with both postures becoming increasingly difficult to
maintain.[1]

Or perhaps increasingly untenable is the better phrase. Since the begin-
ning of the Palestinian uprising in December 1987, but also earlier with the
Israeli invasion of Lebanon in 1982 and the entrenched occupation of the
West Bank and Gaza, Christian and Jewish support for the expansionist
and militaristic policies of the state of Israel can no longer be disguised.
Just as Jews have spoken to Christians of complicity and silence in their
tradition, so too it is increasingly clear that the Jewish people vis-à-vis the
Palestinian people are not innocent either. We as Jews have been and are
today culpable in the suffering of the Palestinian people in the same way
that Christians have been culpable in anti-Jewishness—by portraying Palestinians as less than human, by expropriating their land and property, by
deporting, torturing, and murdering Palestinians, and in the process
attempting to humiliate and destroy them as a people. The ecumenical deal
comes to an end when Christians demand the same critique and source of
action of Jews that Jews demanded of Christians: recognize that you are
no longer innocent, and end the behavior that oppresses another people.[2]

Many Christians are hopefully, one might say anxiously, awaiting an
admission from their Jewish partners of this loss of innocence. But the
essays authored by Jews in this volume illustrate the difficulty of realizing
this hope. When it comes to liberation theology, which always begins with
a critique of one's own people's complicity with injustice and oppression,
and which may, as we shall see later, move Jews and Christians beyond the
impasse that I spoke of earlier, that theology is labeled Christian. It ema-
nates from Latin Americans who suffer poverty and often place the blame
on economic systems that are seen by some Jews as the creative engines of
Western progress. Or they seek to mobilize an unreflective Christian mil-
lenarianism reminiscent of times past where Jews have been persecuted.
The specter of a Christian triumphalism coupled with socialist economics
is enough to anger some Jews who, in the neoconservative political tradition, fear both a resurgent Christianity and a revived socialist possibility
arising from the periphery of Western Christianity and American capitalism.

If these two understandings are present to some extent in the essays of

Norman Solomon and Richard Rubenstein, a more delicate balancing act is constructed by Judd Levingston. He seems to be groping toward the understanding that in relation to Jews and Christians, liberation theology is suggesting more than a particular theological and political platform. Rather it is trying to reinterpret the task of theology from simply commenting on the revealed word of God to creating a framework to nurture the questions a people needs to ask about the history it is creating.[3]

It is instructive that when not confronting a Jewish or Christian liberation theology argument, Rubenstein understands the task of theology as defined above. In fact we might say that Rubenstein, in his analysis of twentieth-century history and the reign of mass dislocation and death at its center, provides the framework for the creation of a liberation theology. To analyze Rubenstein's work is to illustrate the depth of Jewish critical analysis as well as the inability of Jewish theologians to apply this analysis to Third World peoples. Thus what seems at first glance to be almost a diatribe against Jewish and Christian liberation theology yields clues to that which blocks the logical and inevitable future of the ecumenical dialogue.[4]

In his most recent works, *The Cunning of History: Mass Death and the American Future* and *The Age of Triage: Fear and Hope in an Overcrowded World*, Rubenstein emphasizes as the central themes of the twentieth century, in contradistinction with the accolades of progress, the pattern of mass dislocation and mass death. For Rubenstein, the Jewish Holocaust is paradigmatic for our century, in that it shows the capacity of the modern bureaucratic state to render millions of people as superfluous, deprive them of their rights as citizens, segregate them into ghettoes and concentration camps, and ultimately exterminate a now subject population. Rubenstein is relentless in his discussion of mass dislocation and death in the twentieth century as a thoroughly modern exercise in total domination that can be carried out only by an "advanced political community with a highly trained, tightly disciplined police and civil service bureaucracy."[5]

Thus, at the close of the twentieth century, the landscape of dislocation and death forms part of our inheritance. It portends a present and future with horrific possibilities:

There is always the danger that Metropolis will become Necropolis. The city is by nature antinature, antiphysis, and, hence, antilife. The world of the city, our world, is the world of human invention and power; it is also the world of artifice, dreams, charades, and the paper promises we call money. But even the richest and most powerful city can only survive as long as the umbilical cord to the countryside is not cut. Whenever men build cities, they take the chance that their nurturing lifeline to the countryside may someday be severed, as indeed it was in wartime Poland. One of the most frightful images of the death of civilization envisages a time when the city, deprived of the countryside's surplus food and bloated by the countryside's sur-

plus people, feeds upon its own ever-diminishing self and finally col-
lapses. The starving inmates of Auschwitz, consuming their own
substance until they wasted away into nothingness, may offer a prophetic image of urban civilization at the end of its journey from the
countryside to Necropolis. Could it be that as the Jews were among
the countryside's first exiles and among the pioneer inhabitants of
Metropolis, so too they were among the first citizens of Necropolis,
but that, unless current economic, social, and demographic trends are
somehow reversed, there will be other citizens of the city of the dead,
many others?[6]

Rubenstein's analysis of the problematic of twentieth-century life is followed by a prescriptive program that again uses the Jewish Holocaust as
paradigm. As with Hannah Arendt before him, Rubenstein sees the rise of
state power and the ability of that state to exercise domination over its own
citizens — including the ability to deny them their rights as citizens — as the
dilemma that needs to be addressed. Concluding that the history of the
Jews and the twentieth century demonstrate that "rights do not belong to
men by nature" but rather are guaranteed only within the framework of
the political community, and that the secular state has "dethroned all mys-
tifications of power and morality save its own," a new bonding of community
is necessary to minimize the dislocation and death that comes from such
an unstable combination of the person's need for protection and the unlimited power of the state.

It is Rubenstein's view that a "purely secular, rationalistic approach to
our social problems is unlikely to produce the collective altruism our situation demands." Here Rubenstein recounts the formation of the Hebrew
community at Sinai as an example to be emulated in the present. For
Rubenstein, Sinai represents a coming together of a people who shared
neither common origin nor religious inheritance, but who in their oppression and their "common yearning for liberation" sought unity under a single
God. Thus historically the new community was formed by a common religious bond and for Rubenstein this has contemporary relevance: "If we are
to avoid the destructive consequences of our unfolding predicament, either
they or some new encounter with the Sacred will have to fulfill this function
in the period before us."[7]

Thus the Latin American case and the emerging theology of liberation
seem a logical extension of Rubenstein's analysis. Here in the present, tens
of millions of Latin Americans are superfluous to the national and international economic system. For all practical purposes, they exist outside the
protective structures of the state. Though Latin American liberation theology is pluralistic, corresponding to the different contexts in which it is
situated, its main orientation is the inclusion of the poor of Latin America
in the vision of the church and state. God's option for the poor is, in effect,

the assertion of this common religious bond Rubenstein speaks of, which necessitates a politics of inclusion and liberation.

As Gustavo Gutiérrez writes, the task of liberation theologians in the present is intimately linked to the memory of the Jewish Holocaust:

It needs to be realized, however, that for us Latin Americans the question is not precisely "How are we to do theology after Auschwitz?" The reason is that in Latin America we are still experiencing every day the violation of human rights, murder, and the torture that we find so blameworthy in the Jewish holocaust of World War II. Our task here is to find the words with which to talk about God in the midst of the starvation of millions, the humiliation of races regarded as inferior, discrimination against women, especially women who are poor, systematic social injustice, a persistent high rate of infant mortality, those who simply "disappear" or are deprived of their freedom, the sufferings of people who are struggling for their right to live, the exiles and the refugees, terrorism of every kind, and the corpse-filled common graves of Ayacucho. What we must deal with is not the past but, unfortunately, a cruel present and a dark tunnel with no apparent end.

In Peru, therefore—but the question is perhaps symbolic of all Latin America—we must ask: How are we to do theology while Ayacucho lasts? How are we to speak of the God of life when cruel murder on a massive scale goes on in "the corner of the dead"? How are we to preach the love of God amid such profound contempt for human life? How are we to proclaim the resurrection of the Lord where death reigns, and especially the death of children, women, the poor, indigenes, and the "unimportant" members of our society?[8]

Why, then, does Rubenstein, as do other Holocaust theologians like Emil Fackenheim and Irving Greenberg, have such difficulty in logically extending their analysis of suffering and death to Latin Americans, indeed those around the world who are struggling for survival? Why is it that movements of justice are so easily seen as anti-Jewish, as it were the new anti-Semitism? Surely we can see the Palestinians in this light as well: as a displaced people, occupied, without citizenship, segregated. Can we see in the Palestinian people the warning Rubenstein himself applies: "The history of the twentieth century has taught us that people who are rendered permanently superfluous are eventually condemned to segregated precincts of the living dead or are exterminated outright."[9]

The difficulty seems to revolve around the political and theological critique emanating from the theologies of liberation—that is, a critique of European/North American economic and military domination with its attendant links to South Africa and Israel. It reflects as well the possibility of a new and different phase of Jewish and Christian history: the possibility of Jews and Christians struggling together for liberation. The fear is that the state, with the dangerous possibility of unlimited power, may in fact be transformed or undermined, thus inviting anarchy. Though Rubenstein is wary of the power of the state, he is even more afraid of revolutionary movements from the working class and the poor. Religious, especially Christian, legitimation of such movements provide another level of danger: that the institutional church, now seen as a pillar of the social order, will also be swept away.

In effect, though, Rubenstein sees the need for another Sinai. In the modern world it is a Sinai of the middle class, which comes together to stabilize, even humanize, social and political realities that tend toward dislocation and death. The exodus of the nonpersons of the Third World with their own Sinai is feared as holding the possibility of a reign of destruction and death, with the Jews being first in line. Hence the implicit — and often explicit — labeling of these movements on the left, secular and religious, as the new anti-Semitism.[10]

On one level the essays from Latin America in this volume fulfill this expectation. The poor do challenge the international economic system and North American capitalism, and this is stated in startling terms. Pablo Richard refers to North American imperialism as the "worst imperialism of all times." He, along with Julio de Santa Ana and Leonardo Boff, situates the revolutionary struggle of the poor within a further revolution for a Christian theology and a religious institutional presence that addresses the crisis of the poor. They speak of Judaism and the state of Israel within a historical process that Christians are all too familiar with: the growth of a religiosity, linked with economic and political power, in need of critique and transformation.

This is why both de Santa Ana and Richard speak of the common heritage of Jewish and Christian theologies of liberation in the past — for example, the Exodus — and the common links between the two in the present, especially in the critique of unjust power. The further commonality in Judaism and Christianity is the propensity to betray their essential ethical message by becoming in different stages of their history the oppressors. A common project is also proposed — that is, a shared struggle to liberate theology from the propensity toward a conformism to power. Rosemary Radford Ruether, I think, expresses their hope succinctly in the subtitle of her essay: "Toward a Liberation Theology of Jewish-Christian Solidarity."

There is no question that the essays mentioned above are provocative and controversial to Jews and Christians alike. The essential argument that emerges is the authenticity of each faith tradition as it practices solidarity within the present and among the people it shares its life with. Its corollary is the ever-present temptation to betray this solidarity and therefore each tradition's most authentic grounding. Crucial here, from the Christian side, is the first step of self-criticism, and the frequent references to Christendom in Richard's essay represent a summation of this criticism. As he points out, the victims of Christendom, the Jews, deserve a special solidarity. Yet he is also clearly signaling a further victim of Christendom — Christianity itself.

Here Richard addresses Rubenstein's critique of the use of fidelity and betrayal in my own work. Richard is proposing that the question of fidelity and betrayal is not to be seen as one side over against another, as has been the temptation of Christianity and Judaism. Rather, it is to be judged with reference to those impacted by the power emanating from structures of oppression, and whether or not Judaism and Christianity legitimate or critique that power. He further argues that this critique has been common to Jews and Christians from the beginning and that the rejection of that common project by Christendom was possible only by jettisoning the Judaic heritage, which was, at the same time, a rejection of the Christian project as well. Here Richard enters the most controversial realm of Jewish-Christian dialogue, an area extremely controversial within Christianity itself: the birth of Christianity and its relation to the Judaism of its time.

Thus Richard can argue that there is no contradiction between Christianity and Judaism, and that Christianity was not born from the rejection of the Jewish tradition, especially the exilic, messianic, prophetic, and apocalyptic traditions. Rather, Christianity tried to radicalize that tradition. Even more provocative is the statement of Richard's fundamental thesis, that anti-Jewishness does not come from the birth of Christianity, but from the birth of a movement to reject Christianity:

Anti-Semitism is a creation much later than the origins of Christianity — a creation, concretely, of Western Christendom. Moreover, an anti-Semitic rereading of the origins of Christianity was needed to make possible the birth of Western Christendom. Christianity had to be re-created in discontinuity with or in opposition to its biblical-Jewish roots, essentially with exilic, liberation, prophetic, messianic, and apocalyptic traditions. Only an anti-Semitic Christianity could survive in the context of Christendom, a Christianity that will be transformed for centuries into the legitimating ideology of the law and dominating power in the West.

For Richard, the task for Christians becomes clear: recover and reread the origins of Christianity from a perspective prior to Christendom.

It is important to understand that Richard and Ruether, for example, are not counseling a return to a "primitive" or a triumphal Christianity. On the contrary, they argue the recovery of the essential message of Christianity in continuity with its Judaic heritage as a way of addressing its betrayal and entering contemporary reality on behalf of justice, alongside the Jewish people. This is precisely a post-Vatican II and liberationist perspective rather than an attempt to create a new Christendom, even a Christendom pursued for the sake of empowering the poor. Of course the point

of Richard's article and Ruether's work is that Christendom and oppression, thus anti-Semitism, go hand in hand with and feed on each other. In
this symbiotic relationship the Exodus and Jesus become in de Santa Ana's
analysis a comforting memory rather than a disturbing challenge, a claim
of power rather than one of liberation.[11]

The proposed course is one of hope for a future beyond victimization
and oppression, and a liberation of theology from a captivity that threatens
to overwhelm tradition. The statements by Richard regarding the state of
Israel, coupled with his analysis of Christendom, far from being offensive,
take on a positive connotation in the mutual struggle for liberation:

> Both Christianity and Judaism should go back today to their original
> identity, rediscover their original biblical roots, and act in solidarity
> with their own victims. Christians should have solidarity with the vic-
> tims of Western Christendom — in a special way with the Jewish peo-
> ple oppressed by that Christendom. Jews should also have solidarity
> with the victims of the state of Israel — in a special way with the Pales-
> tinian people oppressed by that state. The recovery of our basic orig-
> inal biblical identity through the practice of solidarity is the only
> possible future, for Judaism as well as Christianity. This calls for a
> great humility to recognize our historical errors, especially for us
> Christians, the first to betray our original roots by becoming Chris-
> tendom and by oppressing the Jewish people up to the Holocaust.

Richard then adds that "Christian and Jewish liberation theology, united
in an effective solidarity with the poor and oppressed, is a sign of hope that
it is possible to construct a Christianity beyond Western Christendom, and
to reconstitute Judaism beyond the state of Israel."

Ruether essentially agrees with this analysis by calling Christians and
Jews to a realization of false messianism and the restoration of prophetic
consciousness. Presupposed by both is a "certain trust and confidence in
the truthfulness and goodness of ultimate reality and one's own relation to
it." This recalls de Santa Ana's discussion of bitterness in relation to Jewish
suffering.

Another aspect of the impasse of the Jewish-Christian reality is clearly
marked at this point: Can the feeling of isolation and abandonment felt so
strongly by many Jews be overcome in this Jewish-Christianity solidarity
broached by these essays? Does the journey beyond Christendom and the
state of Israel render vulnerable Jews whose historic experience or vulnerability leaves little to the imagination?

Ruether's analysis seeks to assuage this fear not by pointing out the
goodness of Christians (she in fact does the opposite), but by detailing the
recent empowerment of the Jewish people in Israel and the United States,
and the use of Holocaust scenarios to "terrorize" both Christians and Jews
who dare criticize the state of Israel. Her suggestion that at least in North

America Jews and Christians approach each other as peer communities — having gained and abused power—rather than meeting as victim and victimizer is helpful in outlining an evolving relationship rather than a static historic pattern untrue to the present. If it is true that Christians are no longer innocent, it is also true for Jews.

Perhaps this loss of innocence is the most difficult thing for Christians and Jews to admit, for it challenges the deepest perceptions of our communities and ourselves. Yet it is here that the impasse in ecumenical dialogue may be transcended. To be sure, the loss of innocence can lead to anger and militancy, but it can also open the path of solidarity. To admit culpability is to enter the realm of confession and vulnerability. For Christians it can mean to give up triumphalism and power; for Jews to be healed and to reembrace the beauty of the world. If these essays suggest the difficulty of such an endeavor, they also point to its urgency. We are very nearly too late.

NOTES

1. This ecumenical deal solidified with the victory of Israel in the June 1967 war, which saw on the Jewish side the rise of Holocaust theology and on the Christian side the rise of liberal Christian Zionism. For the initial themes of Holocaust theology, see the writings of Elie Wiesel immediately after the 1967 war in *Against Silence: The Voice and Vision of Elie Wiesel*, vol. 2, Irving Abrahamson, ed. (New York: Holocaust Library, 1985), pp. 187-96. For the need of repentance and the embrace of Israel, see Alice and Roy Eckardt, *Encounter with Israel: A Challenge to Conscience* (New York: Association Press, 1970).

2. For a detailed examination of Israeli policies toward the Palestinian people, see *Punishing a Nation: Human Rights Violations during the Palestinian Uprising, December 1987-1988* (Ramallah, Palestine: Al-Haq/Law in the Service of Man, 1988). Recently, Al Haq shared the Carter-Menil Human Rights Award established by President Jimmy Carter. See "Carter-Menil Rights Award for Israel and Arab Groups," *New York Times* (November 16, 1989), p. 6. For the impact of Palestinian injuries and deaths in proportion to U.S. population figures, see Charles L. Black, Jr., "Let Us Rethink Our 'Special Relationship' with Israel" (September 1989), distributed by the Jewish Committee on the Middle East, Washington, D.C.

3. An unfortunate and typical Jewish response to the suffering of Latin American people is found in Leon Klenicki, "The Theology of Liberation: A Latin American Jewish Exploration," *American Jewish Archives*, 35 (April 1983): 27-39.

4. I am concentrating on Rubenstein rather than Lerner or Waskow because he represents in general major tendencies in Jewish theology and political thought within the Jewish community. For my initial comments on the work of Arthur Waskow, see *Toward a Jewish Theology of Liberation: The Uprising and the Future* (Maryknoll, N.Y.: Orbis, 1989), pp. 49-53. Though I believe that Waskow essentially waffles on the question of Israel, evidently others think him too bold. At the New Jewish Agenda national convention, summer 1989, a resolution was passed in support of Waskow who was "recently fired from the Reconstructionist Rabbinical College due to donor pressures because of his positions on Israel." See Ezra Gold-

stein, "New Jewish Agenda and the Aid-to-Israel Question," *Genesis 2*, 20 (Autumn 1989): 8. For a discussion of Lerner's position, see Marc H. Ellis, *Beyond Innocence and Redemption: Confronting the Holocaust and Israeli Power* (San Francisco: Harper and Row, 1990), pp. 79–82.

5. Richard L. Rubenstein, *The Cunning of History: Mass Death and the American Future* (New York: Harper and Row, 1975), p. 4. Also see his *The Age of Triage: Fear and Hope in an Overcrowded World* (Boston: Beacon Press, 1982). Perhaps it is paradoxical that *The Cunning of History* was written as a response to Rubenstein's exclusion from a major conference on the Holocaust held at the Cathedral of St. John the Divine, June 3-6, 1974. The exclusion was part of a fairly systematic effort to blunt Rubenstein's political and theological critique of the Jewish community during and after the Holocaust. One of the charges was that his theological positions vis-à-vis the God of history and his thoughts on the continuation of the Jewish people after the tragedy of the Holocaust were outside the acceptable range of the Jewish tradition. His willingness to explore the Christian tradition as a partner in dialogue probably did not help in this regard. For his thoughts on Judaism and Christianity, see *After Auschwitz: Radical Theology and Contemporary Judaism* (Indianapolis: Bobbs-Merrill, 1966) and *My Brother Paul* (New York: Harper and Row, 1972). My point here is that Rubenstein's criticisms of *Toward a Jewish Theology of Liberation* carry some of the same themes that he was criticized for as a young theologian!

6. Rubenstein, *Cunning*, p. 95.

7. Ibid., pp. 89, 91. Also see his *Triage*, pp. 232, 237.

8. Gustavo Gutiérrez, *On Job: God-Talk and the Suffering of the Innocent* (Maryknoll, N.Y.: Orbis, 1987), p. 102. Also see his *The Power of the Poor in History* (Maryknoll, N.Y.: Orbis, 1983), pp. 75-110.

9. Rubenstein, *Cunning*, p. 96. At some level Rubenstein does understand the situation, though most often within the context of warring brothers of almost equal strength rather than an empirically powerful Israel vis-à-vis a weak and almost destroyed Palestinian community. Rubenstein writes: "The real damage is that the conflict between the Israelis and the Palestinians will descend into a merciless, uncompromising war to the death." Referring to Meir Kahane's radical demand for the expulsion of Palestinians from the occupied territories, Rubenstein comments to my mind quite accurately: "It would take only one more Arab-Israeli war in which the Israelis emerge victorious for that policy to become official." See Rubenstein, "Covenant and Holocaust," *Remembering for the Future: Jews and Christians During and After the Holocaust* (Oxford: Pergamon Press, 1988), p. 670.

10. See Nathan and Ruth Ann Perlmutter, *The Real Anti-Semitism in America* (New York: Arbor House, 1983).

11. For her ground-breaking work in the area of the relationship of Judaism and Christianity, see Rosemary Radford Ruether, *Faith and Fratricide: The Theological Roots of Anti-Semitism* (New York: Seabury, 1974). Also see her essay, "Beyond Anti-Semitism and Philo-Semitism" in Rosemary Radford Ruether and Marc H. Ellis, eds., *Beyond Occupation: American Jewish, Christian, and Palestinian Voices Paths for Peace* (Boston: Beacon Press, 1990).

Contributors

Leonardo Boff, a Franciscan priest, is a professor of theology in Petròpolis, Brazil. One of the most influential of Latin American liberation theologians, he is the author of such books as *Ecclesiogenesis, Jesus Christ Liberator,* and *Passion of Christ, Passion of the World.* His essay in this volume originally appeared in a special issue of *Christian-Jewish Relations.*

Marc H. Ellis is professor of religion, culture, and society studies at the Maryknoll School of Theology, where he directs the Justice and Peace Program. His books include *Faithfulness in an Age of Holocaust, Toward a Jewish Theology of Liberation: The Uprising and the Future* and *Beyond Innocence and Redemption: Confronting the Holocaust and Israeli Power.*

Judd Kruger Levingston is a Wexner Fellow at the Jewish Theological Seminary Rabbinical School in New York. He has participated in interreligious dialogue with the National Conference of Christians and Jews and with an interreligious discussion group in Jerusalem, B'nai Avraham. His essay was completed while he was the rabbinic intern at the American Jewish Committee, under Rabbi James Rudin.

Otto Maduro, a native of Venezuela, teaches at the Maryknoll School of Theology. He is the author of *Religion and Social Conflict.*

Michael Lerner is a co-founder and editor of *Tikkun* Magazine.

Pablo Richard is a Chilean theologian who teaches at the National University in San José, Costa Rica. His books include *Death of Christendoms: Birth of the Church.*

Richard L. Rubenstein is professor of religion at Florida State University. He is the author of several books including *After Auschwitz: Radical Theology and Contemporary Judaism* and *The Cunning of History: Mass Death and the American Future.*

Rosemary Radford Ruether is Georgia Harkness Professor at Garrett-Evangelical Seminary. Her books have covered such topics as Christian anti-Semitism, liberation theology, and feminist theology. They include *Faith and Fratricide, Sexism and God-Talk, Disputed Questions,* and *The Wrath of Jonah: The Crisis of Religious Nationalism in the Israeli-Palestinian Conflict.*

Julio de Santa Ana is a Protestant theologian from Uruguay. Prominent in the international ecumenical movement, he has served as director of the Committee for the Participation of the Churches in Development of the World Council of Churches. He is currently director of the Ecumenical Center of Services for Evangelization and Popular Education in São Paulo, Brazil.

Dorothee Sölle is a German theologian who has taught widely in Germany and in the United States, where she is also known for her contributions to the peace movement. Her many books include *Of War and Love* and *Revolutionary Patience*.

Norman Solomon is an Orthodox rabbi and director of the Centre for the Study of Judaism and Jewish/Christian Relations at Selly Oak Colleges in Birmingham, England. He serves as editor of *Christian-Jewish Relations*.

Phyllis B. Taylor is a registered nurse and community organizer. She has served on the boards of Amnesty International and the Fellowship of Reconciliation. Currently she coordinates the Witness for Peace Board of Advisors and serves on the Executive Committee of the Jewish Peace Fellowship.

Arthur Waskow was from 1982-89 the editor of *New Menorah*, a journal of Jewish renewal. He is the director of The Shalom Center and the author of *Godwrestling* and *Seasons of Our Joy*.